The Country Houses, Castles and Mansions of
EAST AYRSHIRE

Alex F. Young

Introduction

From the southern edge of Renfrewshire's Uplawmuir in the north, East Ayrshire stretches to the Galloway Forest Park's Loch Enoch in the south; its eastern boundary holding the line of the former County of Ayrshire with Lanarkshire and Dumfriesshire, whilst North Ayrshire and South Ayrshire flank it to the west. Its area of 487 square miles has a population of 120,240 (2010) and, whilst they may think of themselves as being of 'Ayrshire', those in Dunlop know little of Dalmellington – and vice versa.

East Ayrshire Council, with Kilmarnock as its administration centre, is one of Scotland's 32 unitary authorities formed by the Local Government (Scotland) Act 1994 in 1996, having been previously administered as the districts of Kilmarnock & Loudoun and Cumnock & Doon Valley under the 1975 formed Strathclyde Regional Council [Local Government (Scotland) Act 1973].

The castles, mansions and houses featured in this book pre-date these changes.

The castles, including Barr, Caprington, Cessnock, Craufurdland, Loudoun, Rowallan and Sorn, lie mainly in the central belt around Kilmarnock and along the Irvine Valley – whilst many of the country houses across the area owe their existence, or improvement, to money generated by coal, engineering or textiles.

Stenlake Publishing Ltd.

© Alex F. Young, 2017.
First published in the United Kingdom, 2017,
by Stenlake Publishing Ltd.,
54-58 Mill Square,
Catrine, Ayrshire,
KA5 6RD

Telephone: 01290 551122
www.stenlake.co.uk

ISBN 9781840336306

Printed by
P2D Books, 1 Newlands Rd, Westoning, Bedford, MK45 5LD

**The publishers regret that they cannot supply
copies of any pictures featured in this book.**

Acknowledgements

East Ayrshire Council Archives, Burns Monument Centre, Kilmarnock; John Shaw (of Craig); Rebecca Parry / Norman Lawrence on *www.ayrshirehistory.com*; Glasgow Caledonian University Archives – Records of the Scottish Trades Union Congress; Sgt James Platt, Archivist, Scots Guards; The David Sharp Studio, Derby; Prof. Jack Cooper.

Illustration Acknowledgements

Stuart Marshall, 56 (upper); East Ayrshire Council, 6 (upper), 8 (lower right), 9, 10 (both), 23 (bottom), 27 (lower), 28 (upper), 31 (lower), 34 (upper), 46 (lower), 47, 50, 52 (both), 63 (lower), 64, 66 (upper), 80 (lower), 90 (upper), 93 (lower); Duncan & Jane McNaught, 62 (upper); Mr. & Mrs. Arthur Smith, 51 (both); Kenny Baird; 15 (upper), 25 (lower); Simon D Houison Craufurd, 32, 33.

Bibliography

Matthew and George Culley: *Travel Journals and Letters, 1765-1798*, Issue 35.

Michael C Davis, *The Castles and Mansions of Ayrshire*, 1991.

Francis H Groome, *Ordnance Gazetteer of Scotland*, Thos. C. Jack, Grange Publishing Works, Edinburgh, 1885.

T C & E C Jack, *Fairbairn's Book of Crests of the Families of Great Britain and Ireland*, (4th edition), 1905.

John Kay, *A Series of Original Portraits and Caricature Etchings, with Biographical Sketches and Illustrative Anecdotes*, vols. 1 & 2, pub. Hugh Paton, Edinburgh, 1837.

Alexander Hastie Millar, *The Castles and Mansions of Ayrshire, Illustrated in Seventy Views*, pub. William Paterson, Edinburgh, 1885.

David MacGibbon and Thomas Ross, *The Castellated and Domestic Architecture of Scotland*, vols. 1 to 5, pub. Edinburgh, 1887.

James Paterson, *County of Ayr; With a Genealogical Account of the Families of Ayrshire*, vol. I, pub. T G Stevenson, Edinburgh, 1847.

James Paterson, *County of Ayr; With a Genealogical Account of the Families of Ayrshire*, vol. II, pub. Thomas George Stevenson, Edinburgh, 1852.

George Robertson, *Topographical Description of Ayrshire, more particularly Cunninghame, together with a Genealogical Account of the Principal Families*, pub. Cunninghame Press, Irvine, 1820.

Ardnith House, New Cumnock

Built in the 1860s by the Lanemark Coal Company (New Cumnock Collieries from 1910) for their managers, the blonde sandstone Ardnith House stood on a partially wooded three acre site with two access driveways, on the east side of Boig Road, north of Connel Park. Its first occupant, the coalmaster Robert Brown came from Ayr with his family, and was succeeded by his son Thomas Mathieson Brown (b. 1858). Alas, Thomas would not end his days here. On Monday 19th November 1906, the morning post brought a small parcel to Woodside Cottage, Glaisnock Street, Cumnock, home to William Lennox, a 78 year old retired farmer and his housekeeper, 54 year old Miss Grace McKerrow. Posted in Kilmarnock, it contained a cake of shortbread, unprofessionally iced, and a note; *With happy greetings from an old friend.* Four days later Miss McKerrow died from the strychnine later found in the icing, and Brown was arrested for her murder. His wife, Isabella Gibson Proudfoot, was a niece of Lennox. Brown appeared at the Circuit Court at Ayr the following March when, found to be insane and unfit to plead, he was sent to the Criminal Lunatic Department at Perth Prison and died at Ayr District Asylum (Ailsa Hospital from 1958) on 13th November 1915. When the coal industry was nationalised in 1947, Ardnith was occupied for a time by the New Cumnock Collieries general manager, John C George, but fell into decay and was demolished. In 2006 East Ayrshire Council refused a planning application to build a new house on the site.

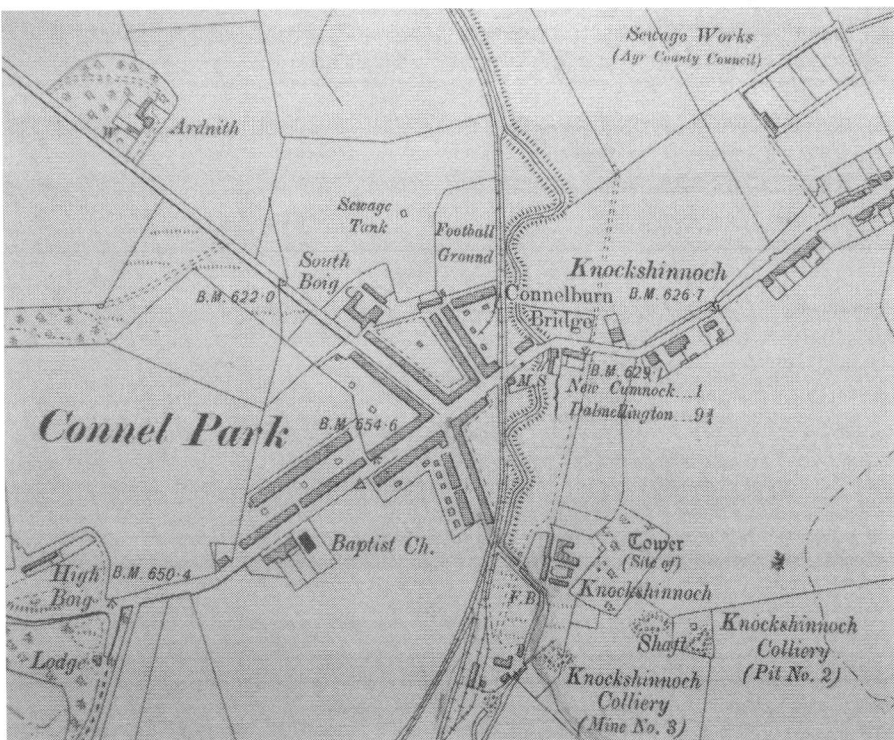

Right: The Ordnance Survey map of 1854-59 showing Ardnith House on Boig Road, north of Connel Park.

Ardoon House, Dunaskin

On the slopes of Green Hill, above Waterside, with a rookery in the trees behind, the Jacobean style Ardoon House was built around 1850 by the newly-established Dalmellington Iron Company (founded by John Houldsworth, 1807-1859), perhaps to drawings by the Edinburgh architect William Burn (1789-1870). Its accommodation of three reception rooms, four bedrooms, kitchen, and servants' quarters, was in sharp contrast to the living conditions of the company's workers in the rows below. The first occupant was Liverpool born John Way Bulkeley (1824-1882), the company's cashier, and his daughter Augusta Alexandra (b. 1844). The photograph dates from 1905 when occupied by James Pettigrew Walker (1856-1912), general manager of the iron works, who had succeeded Bulkeley. The house was an administration centre for the National Coal Board until the 1980s. When the ironworks went into liquidation in 1931 and was taken over by Bairds & Dalmellington Ltd, it expanded the brickworks – built to produce kiln lining bricks for the iron works – and marketed their 'DICO' – Dalmellington Iron Company – bricks until 1976. As a site of industrial archaeological interest, Dalmellington & District Conservation Trust was incorporated in 1985 to restore and preserve the area, including Ardoon House, but when the Trust went into liquidation in 2008, work stopped and the house had its doors and windows boarded.

Assloss House, Kilmarnock

The land, and a fortlet which would form the nucleus of Assloss House, photographed around 1908, is believed to have been granted to Jacob Aucinloss in 1543, and through his descendants to Alexander Montgomery, a Commissioner of Supply for Ayrshire, who died in 1719. In 1725 the Kilmarnock merchant John Glen (1676-1754), bought the estate from the trustees of Montgomery's estate, passing it to his daughter Margaret (b. 1734) who married the Kilmarnock merchant John Parker in May 1754, and hence to their son, William Parker (1755-1822). One of the five founding members (and manager and cashier) of the Kilmarnock Banking Company (1802-1821), William was also the Right Worshipful Master of the masonic lodge St. John Kilmarnock No. 24, when the poet Robert Burns (a member of Lodge St. James, Tarbolton) was made an honorary member in October 1786, and penned the lines; *Ye sons of old Killie, assembled by Willie, to follow the noble vocation*, to mark the occasion. Parker had subscribed to the Kilmarnock Edition of Burns' work, *Poems, Chiefly in the Scottish Dialect*, published on 31st July 1786 by John Wilson of Kilmarnock. The original house became outhouses to this new house, built around 1802. The ornate porch was demolished when the entrance was moved to the rear of the building, and replaced with a window. In 1908 the 170 acre estate was bought by the 8th Lord Howard de Walden, owner of the adjoining Dean Estate, and in 1975 his successor, the 9th Lord, gifted Assloss to the people of Kilmarnock. It is now (2017) Dean Castle Riding Centre, part of Dean Castle Country Park.

John Glen Parker, 'Laird of Assloss and Slidderybraes', shortly before his death in March 1867, aged 78 years. The first child of the banker William Parker and Agnes (daughter of William Paterson of Braehead), who had married the previous year, he was born 8th February 1789 and baptised on 5th March by the Rev. James Robertson of Kilmarnock. In 1808 he sailed to Lisbon, but a career in the wine trade was cut short by the arrival of the invading French. In August 1840 his letter to the *Ayr Advertiser* was re-published by newspapers across the country under the heading; *A Curious Candidate for the House of Commons*. Hoping to stand at the next general election (1841, won by the Conservatives led by Sir Robert Peel) he announced his religious and political creed. *I am warmly, nay enthusiastically, attached to the Church of my forefathers – the Kirk of Scotland, and will spend the last shilling I have in her defence, against all the powers of Hell … . In politics I am an out-and-out double distilled Radical – but take care – no Chartist, or Socialist, the deluded followers of the unhappy Owen* (Robert Owen, 1771-1858), *formerly of Lanark Mills – a man who should have been in a lunatic asylum years ago. I am ashamed to say I am still unmarried, but, under God's grace intend to soon*. He never married, nor gained a parliamentary seat.

Auchinleck House, Auchinleck

Erected between 1756 and 1762 for Alexander Boswell (b. 1707), the 8th Laird of Auchinleck, to succeed the dilapidated, 17th century, 'Place of Auchinleck', an L-shaped fortified house sited to its west. Thomas Boswell, a favourite of King James IV, was granted a charter for the lands in 1504, but both died on Flodden Field nine years later. The architect is unknown, but being contemporary, and similar, to nearby Dumfries House, has been credited, mistakenly, to the Adams. The construction appears to be the work of the Edinburgh builder John Johnston, and as a Senator of the College of Justice, Alexander Boswell (Lord Auchinleck) lived most of the year in Edinburgh's Parliament Square. In 1782 he was succeeded by his son James (1740-1795), the biographer of Samuel Johnson, and in turn by his son Alexander (b.1775), who was killed in a duel near Balburton Farm on the Kirkcaldy to Auchtertool road, Fife in March 1822. Sixteen year old James succeeded his father and in 1830 married Jessie Jane Montgomerie, daughter of Sir James Montgomerie Cuninghame of Corsehill (Stewarton), by whom he had two daughters, the line passing through the second, Emily Harriet, born in 1841. She married Richard Wogan Talbot of Malahide (near Dublin) in 1873. Giving Auchinleck's residents Beechwood Park for a football ground ensured his name lived on with the football team *Auchinleck Talbot*. In the 1920s the estate passed to the Boswells of Garallan, but was abandoned in 1960, and left to decay. Work financed by the Scottish Historic Buildings Trust in 1985 saved it, and in 1999 it was taken over by The Landmark Trust, the 'holidays in historic buildings' charity.

An 1880s photograph of the house from Alexander Hastie Millar's book, *The Castles and Mansions of Ayrshire*. In keeping with the 1985 renovation of the house by the Scottish Historic Buildings Trust, the stables and coach house, to the south of the main house, was renovated by Aly Boswell and her son Rory and opened as *Boswells Coach House*, a coffee house and gift shop, in April 2014.

Two couples under the shadow of a pavilion at the front of the house, perhaps in the autumn of 1909. On the left is Richard Wogan Talbot (1846-1921), 5th Baron Talbot of Malahide, who had married Emily Harriet Boswell, daughter of Sir James Boswell, in June 1873. She died in 1898 and in 1901 he married Isabel Charlotte Blake-Humfrey (seated front left), widow of the Norwich banker John Gurney, who survived him by eleven years. The Judge in the Gilbert and Sullivan comic opera *Trial by Jury* has the line – *At length I became as rich as the Gurneys – An incubus then I thought her* … . To the right, his son James Boswell Talbot (1874-1948), the future 6th Baron, married 28 year old Lucy Joyce Gunning Kerr (1897-1980) in 1924. The other woman is unknown.

Auchmannoch House, Sorn

Standing east of the Galston to Sorn road and north of the Stra' Burn, later named Auchmannoch Burn, the 1856 Ordnance Survey map shows Auchmannoch House with a walled garden to the west and a limestone quarry and limekiln to the east. The crow-stepped gabled "laird's house" has four public rooms and five bedrooms, on three floors, and dates from 1724. The estate passed to Arthur Campbell from the Abbot of Melrose in 1565 – a stone carving of the family crest, a double headed eagle arising from flames, is set into the wall above the entry door. Of equal interest, one of three outbuildings has a window lintel bearing the carving '16 AC MS 94', suggesting it was the home of Arthur Campbell (1633-1703) and his wife Margaret Schaw, (married 1671), and was the original house. The significance of the year 1694 cannot be determined.

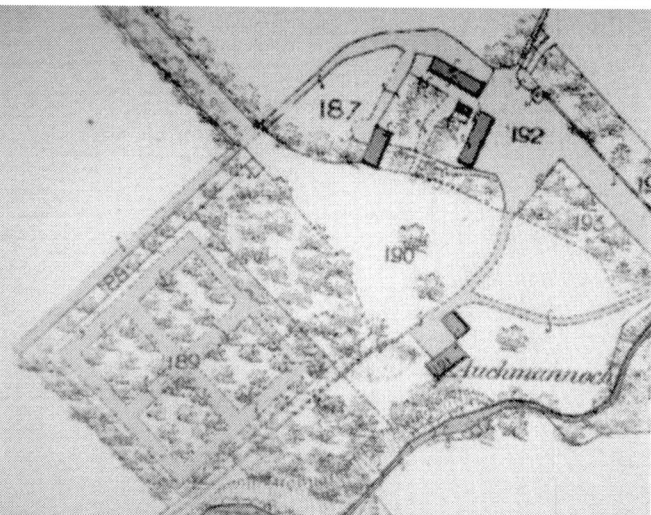

Above, left: The window lintel carving on one of the outbuildings.

Above, right: Auchmannoch estate, on the Ordnance Survey Map (sheet XXIV) of Ayrshire, surveyed in 1856-57 by Captain Bayly of the Royal Engineers, when occupied by Robert Campbell (1782-1857). The building at the top of the map bears the carved window lintel.

Ballochmyle House, Mauchline

Ballochmyle House in the early 1880s when owned by Sir Claud Alexander (1831-1899), created 1st Baronet Alexander of Ballochmyle in February 1886, showing the many additions made to it in the 1830s by his father, Boyd Alexander (1796-1861). The last of the Reid family, which held the estate from the 14th century, was John Reid, an advocate, who spent part of 1720 in Ayr Tolbooth for debt. In the early 1760s Allan Whitefoord (1702-1766) bought the estate and commissioned the Edinburgh architect John Adam (or, perhaps, his brother Robert) to replace Reid's tower-house with this modern building. The son of Sir Adam Whiteford of Blairquhan, he was Cashier for the Royal Bank of Scotland in 1725, a Commissioner of Customs and Excise, and Receiver-General of the Land Tax for Scotland by 1733. On his death the estate passed to his nephew, Sir John Whiteford, who was reduced to penury by the collapse of the Ayr Bank (Douglas, Heron & Co.) in August 1773. In 1783 the estate was bought by Claud Alexander, then in India.

Of the many paintings in the dining room, the largest was the near life size (89 ½ins x 77ins) portrait of Claud Alexander, his brother Boyd (1758-1825), a servant and a Pointer dog. Painted in Calcutta, between September 1783 and February 1784, by the German neo-classical artist Johan Zoffany (1733-1810), Claud holds the letter informing him of his successful purchase of Ballochmyle Estate (£27,600, with rents and timber). Zoffany's other sitters included George III, Queen Charlotte and the Holy Roman Emperor, Francis I, but he was better known in his time for having eaten a sailor who lost a lottery following their shipwrecking off the Andaman Islands in the Indian Ocean. He is remembered, too, in W S Gilbert's libretto for the comic opera *The Pirates of Penzance*, where Major General Stanley admits knowing nothing of modern gunnery, but ... *can tell undoubted Raphaels from Gerard Dow's and Zoffanies* ... . Boyd Alexander served in India from 1776 until 1784, as Deputy-Paymaster to the garrison at Patna, and was MP for Renfrewshire by 1796. Although a number of paintings were auctioned at the house in April 1937, this portrait remained with the family until December 2010, when it was sold at Sotheby's of London for £769,250.

Opposite, below: Building work in progress between 1885 and 1887, under the supervision of the architect Robert Rowand Anderson (1834-1921) of Edinburgh, which gave the house its new front. In a long and distinguished career, which earned him a knighthood in 1902, Anderson designed many churches and schools but contemporary with Ballochmyle, he was also working on Mount Stuart, for the Marquis of Bute; Central Station Hotel, Glasgow and the Scottish National Portrait Gallery, Edinburgh.

The 'new' frontage of the house. With the death of 69 year old Sir Claud Alexander, in London, in May 1899, the family all but severed its links with Ayrshire. The eldest son of Boyd Alexander, Sir Claud was educated at Eton College and Christ Church, Oxford, and as an 18 year old joined the Grenadier Guards with whom he served in the Crimean War (1853-1856), including the Siege of Sevastopol (September 1854-September 1855). Retiring with the rank of major-general he was Member of Parliament for South Ayrshire between 1874 and 1885 and elevated to the Baronetcy in 1886.

An aerial photograph of the house with the hospital extending north-west towards the Mauchline to Catrine road. A number of tenants passed through the estate before October 1939 when it became a 1,200 bed Emergency Medical Services hospital, housed in 32 pavilions, and the house converted to staff accommodation. It closed in 2000, and whilst the pavilions were demolished the house was saved – just. In 2005 Ardgowan Homes (Ballochmyle) Ltd was founded to develop the estate, with the building of 94 houses and the renovation of the mansion to hold fourteen flats. Work on the main house was completed, but the company was dissolved in November 2014 with the project incomplete.

The West Lodge entrance to the estate, on the Mauchline to Catrine road, in the late 1880s when it was home to the estate's forester Alexander Donald. The woman to the right is thought to be his Stirlingshire born wife Janet *née* Douglas, holding their daughter Mary (b.1885). The lodge and gateway were contemporary with the 1885 work on the main house but, despite being a category C listed building, seem to have fallen down around 2008, whilst development work was progressing. Today (2017) it is a one metre high rubble filled base.

Sir John Whitefoord (1734-1803) of Ballochmyle and Whitefoord is the centre figure in this 1785 etching from John Kay's *Edinburgh Portraits*, flanked (on the left) by Major Andrew Fraser (d.1795) and The Honourable Andrew Erskine (d.1793), with Miss Margaret Burns (d.1792), who kept a house of ill-repute in Rose Street, and Meg Murray, who kept a lodging house in Shakspeare Square, Edinburgh.

Bank House, New Cumnock

Neither the inspiration for its Italianate design, nor its architect are known, but Bank House was built in the 1840s for John Hyslop (1818-1878) of Bank, a 279 acre estate, with its entry on the south side of the New Cumnock to Dalmellington road, opposite High Boig, which he also owned. The Hyslops were from Blackcraig, a small farm close to the Langlee Burn, a tributary of the Afton Water. The Rev. Matthew Kirkland of New Cumnock writes in the *Statistical Account* of 1838 that William (father of John), who died in 1852 – *deserves honourable notice as a spirited enterprising agriculturalist having, the previous year, won the premium for the best managed farm in Kyle*. However, it was the coal beneath Bank estate that brought the family wealth, John founding the Bank Coal Company around 1860. In 1909 his son William, 'Laird of Bank', formed New Cumnock Collieries Ltd., bringing together the pits of the Bank Coal Company and the failed Lanemark Coal Company. He died in 1936, aged 81 years. The roof of Bank House was removed in the early 1960s and the remaining structure demolished in the 1980s.

Barr Castle, Galston

An early 1900s view along Wallace Street towards Barr Castle, or 'Lockhart's Tower', with the 1859 built United Presbyterian Church (by the Edinburgh architects Peddie and Kinnear) on the right. On a base measuring 48 feet by 35 feet the five storey castle was built by the Lockhart family of Barr between 1400 and 1452, passing to the Campbells of Cessnock in the 1670s and, later, to the Duke of Portland.

The wool-spinner Hugh Richmond of Galston's Bentinck Street was the castle's last commercial tenant before William John Arthur Charles James Cavendish-Bentinck, 6th Duke of Portland (1857-1943), through his factor, Brother James Harling Turner, granted the castle to Galston's Masonic Lodge, St. Peter 331 in 1894, on a rent of £2 per annum, gifting it to them in 1922. They had previously met in the Portland Arms Hotel in Cross Street. The work of converting the ground floor to a lodge, at a cost of £210, was carried out by local tradesmen – Robert Anderson, mason, Clinchyard Farm; James Holburn, joiner, Wallace Street; James Frew, gasfitter, Station Road, and Robert Torrance, painter, of Cross Street. The consecration ceremony was conducted by Thomas Horatio Arthur Ernest Cochrane (1857-1951), the Right Worshipful Provincial Grand Master of Ayrshire, the Unionist Member of Parliament for North Ayrshire (1892-1910) and future (1919) 1st Baron Cochrane of Cults. It remains the oldest building in the world to hold Freemasonry meetings. The photograph dates from 1913.

Barskimming House, Mauchline

The neo-Georgian style Barskimming House around 1902 when owned by Sir William Frederick Miller, 5th Baronet of Glenlee (1868-1948). It had been re-built in 1883 under the supervision of the Edinburgh architect Charles Reid (1828-1883), following the loss of its predecessor – built for Sir Thomas Miller (1735-1816), Lord Glenlee, President of the Court of Session, in 1771 – to a fire. The estate's grain mill, powered by the River Ayr, was lost to a fire in 1892, and also re-built. The 3,755 acre Barskimming estate with thirteen farms, two smallholdings, 500 acres of woodland and sandstone and honestone quarries, straddled the River Ayr to the south-west of Mauchline, dated from 1377 when King Robert II granted the lands of Barskymyn to William Rede, who built a fortalice. In December 1913, when offered for sale at a public roup in the Hall of the Faculty of Procurators in Glasgow, it was bought by Major (1st Lanarkshire Volunteers) Robert Jack Dunlop of Thomas Dunlop & Co., the Glasgow grain and shipping merchants. He died at the house in 1938, aged 80 years.

The burnt out shell of Barskimming House following the fire which broke out in the early hours of Wednesday, 8th March 1882. Starting in a ground floor pantry, it spread upwards through the house, sending the tenant, Archibald Buchanan of Catrine Cotton Works, and his wife and servants, to safety in their night-attire. Fire engines from Catrine Works and Mauchline were too late to be effective, especially as the hoses for their pumps were not long enough to reach the river. Some furniture and fittings, replaced when the house had been renovated two years earlier, were saved, but the Buchanan's family silver was lost. Of the total loss of £180,000, £10,000 was insured. The Millers were unfortunate with destructive house fires. Sir William Frederick Miller was living in Englemere Lodge, near Ascot Racecourse, Berkshire, when it was destroyed by fire in the early hours of 7th March 1907.

The estate's staff on the bridge around 1910, when their employer was the Newcastle-upon-Tyne brewer, John Meikle (1833-1913). Individuals cannot be named but amongst them would have been: Christine Shonach (35), parlourmaid; Margaret Wightman (28), housemaid; Christina Monroe (19), kitchenmaid and the 38 year old cook,

Ellen Bremner. The single arch, red ashlar sandstone bridge, with its four obelisks, was built in the 1780s, some 90 feet above the River Ayr. In his 1790s Statistical Account of Machlin, the Rev. Mr. William Auld wrote – *there are several useful bridges near Machlin, particularly the new-bridge at Barskimming; built by the late Sir Thomas Miller. It excels all the bridges of the county in beauty and elegance, and is one of the greatest curiosities to be seen in it.*

A steel line engraving of an idyllic scene on the River Ayr, looking upstream towards the bridge, with Barskimming House in the top left. The engraving is by William Richardson (Edinburgh Directory, 1846; 3 Francis Place, Edinburgh), from a work by the Scottish painter David Octavius Hill (1802-1870), for the two volume book, *The Works of Robert Burns, with Numerous Notes and Illustrations*, published by Blackie & Son, London, in 1853.

Sir William Miller of Glenlee (1755-1846). (Kay's Edinburgh Portraits). The only son of Sir Thomas Miller (1717-1789), President of the Court of Session, Sir William was admitted to the Faculty of Advocates in 1777 and promoted to the bench in 1795 as Lord Glenlee, taking the name from the family's estates in Galloway. Although Barskimming was his home, when the court in Edinburgh was in session he lived in Brown's Square – later absorbed into Chambers Street – walking to court each morning, under his freshly powdered wig, with his cocked hat in hand. This Kay etching dates from 1799 when Miller was 44 years of age. In 1778 he had married a cousin, Grizel Chalmers by whom he had six sons and three daughters. His second son, Lieut.-Colonel William Miller of the First Foot Guards fell at the Battle of Waterloo on 18th June 1815. Sir William retired from the Court of Session in 1840 and died at Barskimming in May 1846.

Bellfield House, Riccarton

Bellfield House in the summer of 1921 when the 240 acre estate, with its house and walled garden, was administered by the Buchanan Bequest Trustees – the provost, magistrates and ministers of Kilmarnock and Riccarton – on behalf of the community. Built in the late 18th or early 19th century by the Fairlies of Holms, Galston – James Fairlie, one time merchant of Kingston, Jamaica, and a partner in the Kilmarnock Banking Company, died here in May 1819. It was bought in the early 1840s by the Misses Buchanan; Margaret (1793-1864), Jane (1796-1867) and Elizabeth (1803-1875), following the death of their father George Buchanan (1755-1840), a merchant, of Woodlands House, Glasgow. On Elizabeth's death on 23rd April 1875, as agreed by the sisters, the estate – valued in excess of £100,000 – was divided into bequests, including Bellfield Estate. Initially, part of the house was a home for the district's aged and infirm and the library was retained for public reference, but it was later removed to the Dick Institute, Kilmarnock, where oil portraits of the sisters are also held. In June 1952 Kilmarnock Town Council took 229 acres of the policies for a housing scheme of 1,859 houses, flats and shops – today's Bellfield (*Glasgow Herald*, 12th June 1952) – and in January 1969 relieved the trust of responsibility for the house and the remaining eleven acres. A survey of the building found signs of settlement, distortion of the roof and cracks in the external walls, whilst the interior was infested with dry rot, wet rot and woodworm and, having no further worthwhile purpose, was demolished. West of the house stand three Monkey Puzzle (Araucaria araucana) trees, planted in memory of the sisters.

Griffin-topped pillars support an ivy-covered arch over the path from the walled garden to the house – just visible through the trees on the right. The photograph dates from 1921 but it is not known when the arch was built – or removed.

The walled garden in the 1920s. When Kilmarnock Town Council relieved the Buchanan Trust of the remaining eleven acres of the estate in 1969, there were plans for a pitch and putt golf course, tennis courts, football pitches and, within the walled garden, a bowling green. Local landscape contractor Mitchell & Struthers cleared and levelled the garden and laid turf in time for Bellfield Bowling Club, with Jimmy Robb as president, to open for the 1974 season.

Bellsbank House, Dalmellington

Bellsbank features on Armstrong's 'new map of Ayrshire' of 1775, as two buildings, named Bilsbank, but there is no record of either an architect, or builder. When this photograph of the north face of the house, on the approach from Dalmellington, was taken in 1905 it was occupied by sheep farmer William Dykes. Its earliest occupant appears to have been David Woodburn (d.1822), when factor to Quintin M'Adam of Craigengillan. The house stood on 690 acres of moorland – extending from the head of Loch Doon to Patna – sustaining up to 20,000 sheep and remained part of Craigengillan estate until 1919 when it was bought by John Walker of Polquhairn.

Braehead House, Kilmarnock

Braehead House in 1903 when occupied by James Middleton, factor to Lord Howard de Walden's estates. The architect is unknown but it was built around 1765 for the lawyer, and Kilmarnock's town clerk, William Paterson (1718-1772), who proclaimed to the town's people the ascension of King George III in 1760. The driveway followed the line of today's Braehead Court, from London Road, with the house overlooking the Kilmarnock Water and, from 1827, Kilmarnock Bowling Club's green, development having forced it from its original site between East and West George Street. Founded in 1740 it is the United Kingdom's oldest surviving bowling club. In 1819 the house and its grounds were in the hands of the Duke of Portland and occupied by a succession of his estate factors, including George Kelk who died in 1857. The grounds extended east, to where Kilmarnock College stood on Holehouse Road (Hollis Road in the 1850s) and de Walden Terrace built around 1895. It was demolished in 1966 and by 1970 work was progressing on the houses of Braehead Court.

The Braes, Darvel

In 1891 the lace and madras manufacturer Alexander Jamieson (1853-1923) of Darvel bought land on the east side of Burn Road from Baron Donington (Charles Frederick Abney-Hastings of Loudoun) and, between 1898 and 1902, had this house built for himself, his wife Margaret and their family. His mill was at the junction of Burn Road and West Donington Street (now Lace Mill Wynd and Lacemill Garden), trading as Alexander Jamieson & Company, with another on Glasgow's Montrose Street. Prior to moving to the Braes, the family resided on Glasgow's Onslow Drive.

From modest beginnings, with seventeen madras (cotton fabric) looms, his Darvel mill expanded to over 200 looms employing 300 workers. Overseas business would eventually be handled through an office in London's Newgate Street. From 1893 until his death in 1923 he was Chief Magistrate – 'Provost' – of Darvel, and awarded an MBE in 1909 in recognition of his work for the community. Of the couple's four sons and three daughters, two died in the First World War; Captain Nicol Jamieson, of the Royal Scots Fusiliers, killed in action at Gallipoli in August 1915, and Lieutenant William Patterson Jamieson, of the Heavy Machine Gun Corps, who died on the Western Front in April 1917. This 1920s photograph shows the original house, with a conservatory on the left and the kitchen area to the right.

By the 1930s Jamieson's mill was attracting businessmen from around the world and the family added the bedroom extensions to either side to accommodate them – the bedroom doors still bear room numbers.

Busbie Castle, Knockentiber

The ruined Busbie Castle, from the south, around 1904, with the hamlet of Knockentiber stretching behind, on the Crosshouse to Kilmaurs road. The building on the left, with the dormer windows, is the 1870 built Tiber Tavern. The Ordnance Survey map of 1856 shows, also, the site of a pre-Reformation chapel, dedicated to the Virgin Mary, to the west of the castle, whilst the ground to the right slopes down to the Carmel Water. Standing 50 feet high, the castle comprised of three storeys, on a base measuring 40 feet by 25 feet, and was probably built by David Mowat who held a charter on the lands between 1390 and 1406. Recorded history passed it by – it was a ruin when Andrew Armstrong mapped the area in 1775 – and it only came to notice in June 1949 when, due to its ruinous and crumbling condition it was considered a danger. The options were to restore it at a cost of £1,500 or demolish it – but the money could not be found.

Camlarg Lodge, Dalmellington

Until its demolition in the late 1940s, Camlarg Lodge stood amidst trees on the south side of the road to New Cumnock, this 1920s photograph showing the early 19th century house, with later extensions to either side. It was very different to the tower house known to Johne Craufurd, who died here in the spring of 1579, and his son, William Crawford, who attempted to establish a glass manufactory around 1616. In 1741 it was bought by William Logan (b.1739), a director of the banking house Douglas, Heron & Company of Ayr and Dumfries, but when the bank collapsed, in June 1772, Logan's estate was sequestrated and in July 1778, the 600 acre estate was sold to John McAdam of Craigengillan for a pittance. There were a number of tenants including; David Woodburn, late of the Honourable East India Company Service (d.1821) and his descendants, and James Baird Thorneycroft of Netherplace, Mauchline, who used it as a shooting lodge, until it was commandeered by the War Office in June 1916 to accommodate the officers attached to the Loch Doon School of Aerial Gunnery. It was part of Craigengillan when the estate was advertised for sale in December 1918 by Mrs. Charlotte Tilke McAdam, but whilst the other properties sold quickly, Camlarg was a ruin when bought by the Dalmellington Iron Company in August 1940.

Caprington Castle, Riccarton

The family name Cuninghame has been synonymous with Caprington estate since the 14th century, when the land – then known as Baidland – was granted to Thomas, 3rd son of Sir William Cunynghame, and confirmed by a charter from his elder brother William, on 9th August 1385. The fortalice *Caprintoun*, with the church at *Ricardtoun* to its east, appears on a manuscript map of *Cuningham* by the cartographer Robert Gordon of Straloch (1580-1661) published between 1636 and 1652. The three storey, 15th century, building, on a base measuring 48 feet by 33 feet, was modernised in 1797 by Sir William Cuninghame. The 1791 Tax Rolls show he had three male servants – gardener, groom and servant, and two female servants, whilst the Rolls for 1797 record seven dogs and four timepieces; one clock, two gold watches and one of silver. Sir William inherited the estate on the death of his father, Sir John Cuninghame in 1777, but having no heirs at his death in 1829, aged 77 years, the estate passed to his cousin Sir Robert Keith Dick of Prestonfield, who assumed the name Cuninghame. A remodelling later that year, by the architect Patrick Wilson of Edinburgh, produced the house in today's form and style.

A sketch of the north-east front of the castle showing the 1797 additions made for Sir William Cuninghame, perhaps from the plans drawn by the mason and architect David Henderson of Edinburgh around 1780, but who had died in 1789.

FIG. 1352.—Caprington Castle. View from North-East.

The East Lodge, or Ivy Lodges (OS map 1910), entry to Caprington Estate on the west side of Ayr Road in 1902 (now opposite Caprington Avenue), when occupied by John Garrick, a 69 year old general carter and his wife Margaret. Probably contemporary with the 1820s re-build of the castle, it was on that part of the estate given over to the adjacent Caprington Colliery; the 1881 census shows it occupied by John Samson, colliery engine keeper. It was a house divided, the living room and kitchen being in the left side and the bedroom on the right, and appears to have been demolished in preparation for the building and opening – 1st June 1968 – of Caprington Golf Club's new clubhouse.

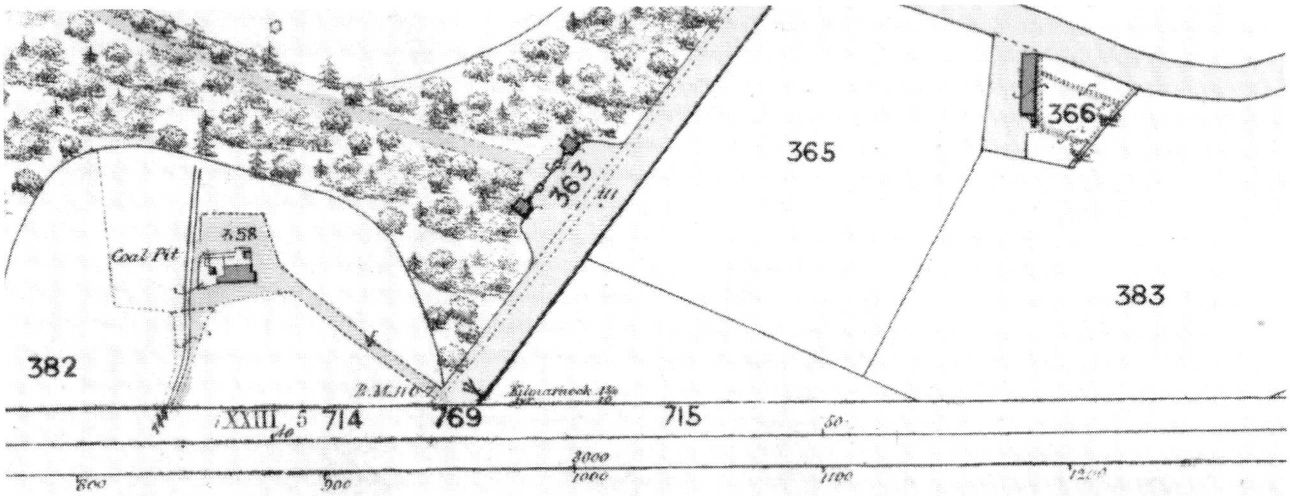

The Ordnance Survey map (Ayr, sheet XXIII.1, 1854) showing the East Gate and Caprington Coal Pit.

Carskeoch House, Patna

Carskeoch House in the early 1900s when occupied by William Murray Samson Howatson, sheep farmer, who died at Auchenflower House, Ballantrae, in July 1915, aged 63 years. The earliest record of the property is a 1671 testament dative of Glasgow Commissary Court, relating to Thomas Thomsone, who had died intestate. The core of the house in the illustration was probably built for Andrew McCosh around 1796, when he married Jane Carson and by whom he had five daughters and one son, James. Born in March 1811, James was ordained a minister and appointed to Brechin, from where he was invited to be president of Princeton College (now University), New Jersey, U.S.A., serving from 1868 until 1888 and dying there in 1894. By 1851 the 400 acre Carskeoch was home to Henry Montgomery-Cuninghame, son of Sir James Montgomery-Cuninghame of Corsehill, Stewarton. Having resigned from the 29th Regiment of Foot as a lieutenant, he joined the Ayrshire Militia Rifles as a captain. A bachelor, he died in May 1883, aged 68 years, his death certificate giving his occupation as *Proprietor of Mining and other shares*; his portfolio contained investments in the Caledonian Railway Company, the Highland Railway Company, the Glasgow Tramway and Omnibus Company and the India Rubber Gutta Percha and Telegraph Works. Bought by the Duke of Portland it was tenanted by Howatson, but was one of nearly 90 properties sold by the Duke in 1919. When sold by the Forestry Commission in 1974 its policies had fallen from 329 acres to 48 acres of hill, eleven acres of woodland and two and a half acres of garden.

Nether Catrine House, Catrine

In 1997 Nether Catrine House, on the Newton Street (Stewart Place) – Townhead corner was incorporated into a new-build crescent of housing for LFK Investments of Paisley – the only indication of its history being a datestone, *AA HR 1682* (extant), set into the north face (the rear of the original building). The lettering style suggests this to be a copy of the original 'AA MD 1687', recording the marriage of Adam Aird to Margret Dalrimple at Mauchline on 16th June 1687. Adam Aird probably built the house, the land having been bought by a forebearer, William Aird in 1593. The photograph shows the building's south facing front. By the late 18th century it was the summer retreat of Dugald Stewart (1753-1828), Professor of Moral Philosophy at Edinburgh University – his Edinburgh addresses included Hay's Street and Lothian House on Canongate. In 1831, the nine column Dugald Stewart Monument, by the architect William Henry Playfair, was erected on Edinburgh's Calton Hill. In October 1786 Stewart hosted a dinner to the poet Robert Burns – *Where Burns dinner'd wi' a Lord* – and Lord Daer, the second son of the 4th Earl of Selkirk. The Stewarts moved to their newly-built Catrine House above Howford Bridge around 1820, but retained, and rented, the old house. Amongst its many tenants was Alexander Greenshield (1806-1844) of Catrine Brewery, St. Germain Street who, in April 1839, sub-let it to the newly formed congregation of the United Secession Church. On the death of Colonel Mathew Stewart in 1851, aged 66 years, it was bought by Arthur Campbell (1788-1875), Writer to the Signet, son of Arthur Campbell of Auchmannoch, and remained with the Campbell family until 1909. It was a farmhouse for a number of years, John T Dowie & Son's garage for a few more and in July 1989 added to the Secretary of State's list of buildings of special architectural or historic interest.

Where Burns dinner'd wi' a lord

The house in its early 20th century days as a farm.

Catrine House, Catrine

With the village of Catrine losing its pastoral character to Finlay's cotton mill, the Stewarts bought, initially, 50 acres of land adjacent to the Goat Inn on the Mauchline–Auchinleck road, south of Howford Bridge around 1820 and built this new 'Catrine House', with its woodland clothed slope running to the south bank of the River Ayr. The estate later extended to over 300 acres, with the addition of the farms of Catrine, Catrineshaw, Merkland and Barwhillan. Following the death of Lt-Col Mathew Stewart in 1851 the contents of the house were sold at auction and, with Nether Catrine House, bought by Arthur Campbell of Auchmannoch. The house was demolished in the 1940s, and since 2006 its site occupied by the timber-built, Catrine House Ice Cream Parlour.

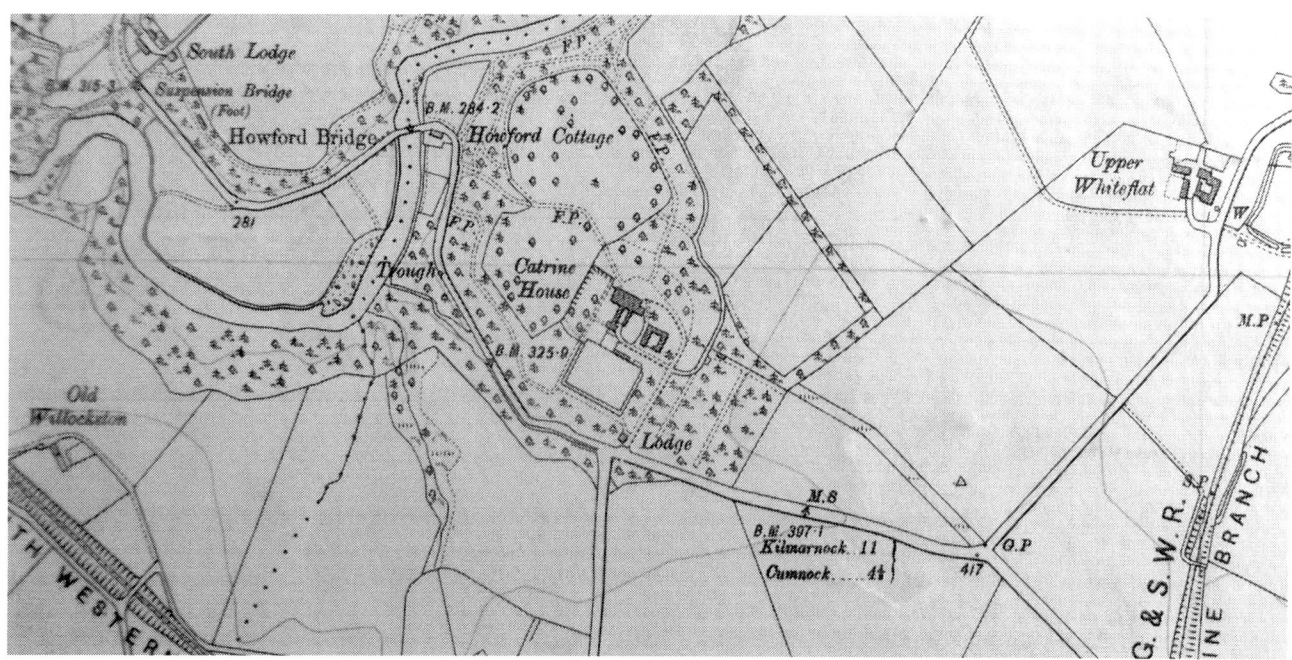

Catrine House on the 1854 Ordnance Survey map.

The lodge house on the Cumnock to Mauchline road around 1900, when occupied by the estate's gardener, George Stewart (b. Blair Athole, 1854), his wife Annie (b. Bonhill, Dunbartonshire, 1856) and their sons, Peter and George. It is probably contemporary with the main house, but is now clothed with rendering, in a changed scene. Gone is the backdrop of mature trees and most of the main gate, and gone too is the passing traffic since the opening of the new Howford Bridge in September 1962.

Cessnock Castle, Galston

Cessnock Castle in Edwardian times when owned by the 6th Duke of Portland, William John Arthur Charles James Cavendish-Bentinck (1857-1943). On the right is the 14th century 'Tower of Galliestoun' – hence Galston – topped with the belfry taken from Galston Parish Church when it was rebuilt in 1808. Sixteenth and 17th century extensions, with stones dated 1675 and 1680, form today's courtyard. From the late 13th century it was owned by Sir John Keith, one of those in the failed attempt to take the heart of Robert the Bruce to Jerusalem for burial, in

1330 – says legend. When Alexander Hume (1675-1740), 2nd Earl of Marchmont, married Margaret, daughter of Sir George Campbell of Cessnock in 1697, he took the name Campbell, and the restoration of the castle, evidenced by a series of letters (held by the Scottish Records Office) he exchanged with John Dick, the estate's factor, between 1723 and 1727. The work ranged from the removal and rebuilding of walls, the installation of new windows, and the planting of trees and shrubs in the grounds. In the 1770s it was acquired by John Wallace of Cairnhill (Carnell) and a decade later by the 3rd Duke of Portland, whose family (later Welbeck Estate) owned it until 1939 – the last occupant being their factor, Joseph Harling Turner – when it was sold to Robert Conroy-Robertson (b.1908), (Baron de Fresnes by deed poll in 1944), who had married Fiona Huddleston Abney-Hastings, daughter of Reginald Mowbray Chichester Abney-Hasting, Marquess of Loudoun, in 1940. Fresnes, having served as a captain in the Royal Artillery, ran the house as an hotel and the base for his antiques business. In 1981 he sold part of the property, and on his death, in February 1995, the remainder was sold.

Joseph Harling Turner (1859-1942). Born at Dean Castle, Kilmarnock, and educated at the town's academy, Joseph's father, Frederick John Turner (1824-1906), was factor to the Duke of Portland's estates in England before moving from Mansfield Woodhouse in Nottinghamshire to Kilmarnock, around 1858, to manage the Duke's Ayrshire and Caithness properties. In 1875 Joseph joined his father in the management of the estate, and in 1883 married 20 year old Mary Jane Adam at Closeburn Castle, where her father John Adam was factor, setting up home at Cessnock Castle. When the Local Government (Scotland) Act of 1889 created county councils, he represented Kilmarnock, and was convenor of Ayrshire County Council between 1924 and 1931. He was a founding member, and first captain, of Ossington Golf Club, which played over a nine hole course on Holms Farm, Kilmarnock, before moving to the coast to become Kilmarnock (Barassie) Golf Club in 1894 – on Portland estate land. His work as an adviser on government agricultural policy during the First World War earned him a CBE in January 1918. A life governor of the West of Scotland Agricultural College he was instrumental in establishing the Kilmarnock Dairy School at Holms Farm and its later move to Auchencruive as the Hannah Dairy Research Institute. In the late 1930s, when a widower, he moved from Cessnock Castle to the House of Craigie, previously the parish manse but then owned by the Portland estate, where he died in January 1942.

Corsehill Castle, Stewarton

Resembling an overgrown tombstone, between the Dunlop road and the railway line, north of Stewarton, is the single wall remnant of Corsehill Castle. This 1902 photograph, taken from the south-east, shows the inside of the west wall, with a first floor fireplace. The castle belonged to the Cuninghames, and whilst the Ordnance Survey Name Book for Ayrshire was being researched in 1855, Sir Thomas Montgomery-Cuninghame, the 8th Baronet (c.1808-1870), told the surveyors the ruin dated from the 1540s (possibly built by William, 4th Earl of Glencairn, who died 1547), and was last occupied in the late 18th century, by John, the 15th Earl, who died unmarried in 1796.

Craig House, Kilmaurs

Craig House, north-west of Gatehead, beyond Milton Mill, survives thanks to a cross-subsidy development approved by East Ayrshire Council in 2001, whereby Chardon Homes (West of Scotland) Ltd. of Callander (dissolved 2006) would renovate and convert the then roofless Craig House into eleven residential units and erect fourteen houses in the grounds, at a cost of £1.1 million. The estate was owned by John Glasgow (d.1764), a timber and slate merchant, and Provost of Irvine between 1742 and 1751, and came to the marine Captain John Morrice (1743-1788), through his marriage to Glasgow's daughter Elizabeth in 1780. The line passed through their son, Robert Morrice of Craig (d.1827) and from him to William Pollock, an army surgeon, who took the surname Pollok-Morris and died in 1862, aged 78 years. He commissioned the architect James Ingram to add the portico in the 1830s but the family's connection with the house ended on the death of Colonel William Pollok-Morris, of the 18th Hussars, in September 1936. It was commandeered by the War Department during the Second World War and Glasgow Corporation (later Strathclyde Regional Council) used it as a children's home until 1989.

Craigengillan House (Berbeth House), Straiton

Berbeth House from Corson's Knowe in the 1890s when it was the centre of the 28,500 acre Craigengillan estate, comprising of 20 sheep farms and holdings, with Alexander Frederick McAdam (1864-1901) as laird. On the left, with its entry through the candle snuffer domed tower, is the stable block, with granary and workshops, and the house to the right. On Robert Gordon's map *Cuningham* (1636-52) the house is named Barbeth (later Berbeth), and only given the name Craigengillan, from the estate, in the early 20th century, by Alexander's widow, Charlotte Tilke McAdam *née* Mills (1854-1952), whom he had married in London in 1886.

The history of the McAdam family is uncertain but, having come from Waterhead in Carsphairn, Kirkcudbrightshire, appear to have been granted the beginnings of Craigengillan estate by a Crown Charter of 1611. The original, thatched, house would have been to the right in this view, which John McAdam (d.1790) remodelled in the 1770s. He appears in the Carriage Tax Roll for 1788, paying £7.0.0 that year for his 4 wheeled carriage.

In December 1918 Mrs. Charlotte Tilke McAdam put the estate into the hands of the Hanover Square, London based 'valuations, surveying and auction' company, Knight, Frank and Rutley, and was bought by Alexander Gavin, manager of the Dalmellington Iron Company from 1906-1920, remaining with his family until 1999. This image dates from the 1950's.

The gatehouse at the estate entry off the Dalmellington to Ayr road, in the 1950s. Its distinctive ogee headed windows suggest it may date from around 1804, when Quintin McAdam made additions to the main house. It appears on John Thomson's map of 1828.

Contemporary with the lodge is the bridge taking the carriageway to the main house over the Muck Water, having passed under McClymont's Bridge in Dalmellington, on its way to join the Cumnock Burn and the River Doon. The stonework and the bridge railings have been renovated since this 1950s photograph.

Craufurdland Castle, Kilmarnock

The Eglinton Hunt at Craufurdland Castle in the early 1920s when Lt. Col. William Reginald Houison Craufurd of the Argyle & Sutherland Highlanders was Laird. He died on 28th February 1925. The history of Craufurdland, or Ardach as it was, begins in the 13th century with the marriage of Sir Reginald de Craufurd of Clydesdale, Sheriff of Ayr, to the heiress of the Loudoun estates. Their grandson John Craufurd became the first Laird of Craufurdland. Generation succeeded generation until 1793. On his death-bed, Lt. Col. John Walkinshaw Craufurd, who had distinguished himself at the Battle of Dettingen (1743) when a British force defeated the French, settled the estate on his friend, the London banker, Thomas Coutts. His aunt, Elizabeth Craufurd, raised a civil action to retain the estate which, after her death in 1802 (aged 97 years) was continued by her son-in-law the Rev. James Moody, and won in a House of Lords appeal in 1806, restoring Craufurdland to the family. The Rev. Moody of Perth and Elizabeth 'Betty' Houison were married at Cramond Church in November 1777 – he assuming the name James Houison Moody Craufurd – by the Rev. Robert Walker, the subject of the 1790s painting, *The Rev. Robert Walker Skating on Duddingston Loch, (The Skating Minister)* by Sir Henry Raeburn. The Ordnance Survey Name Book (1855) records; *This Castle stands near the edge of a steep bank which rises from the Craufurdland Water. The part, called the Old Tower, is of a rectangular shape and forms the south-western extremity of the building, its date is unknown, but supposed to be about 500 years old. The East wing was erected in 1648, the Front in 1811, the drawing room portion in 1836 and the remainder in 1838 and 1847. The present occupier is William Howieson Craufurd, Esqr, from whom this information was obtained.* The building's coat of ivy has come and gone, but its only structural change, since 1847, has seen the removal of the two frontal chimneys in the 1960s.

Three generations of the Craufurd family at the entry to the castle in the late 1860s. From the left is William Houison Craufurd, his granddaughter Constance, and his daughter-in-law Mary, with the estate's gamekeeper. The son of James Houison Moody Craufurd and Elizabeth, William was born at Perth around 1782 and on the death of his mother, in April 1823, succeeded to the estate. In 1808 he married Janet Esther Whyte (d.1856) who bore his son and successor John Reginald Houison Craufurd in 1811 (d.1887). In 1847 John married Mary Dundas Hamilton (d.1878), fifth daughter of John Hamilton of Sundrum, at Mount Charles, near Ayr. Born in Nice, France, Constance Mary Houison Craufurd, their third daughter, died, unmarried, at Crosbie West, Newton Stewart in April 1935.

Crofthead Cottage, Muirkirk

Muirkirk's Kirkgreen runs north off Main Street, turning left into Wellwood Street as the road to Tardoes Farm and Crofthead Cottage swings right around the old graveyard. The farm is noted in the 1797 Farm Horse Tax Rolls when Francis Howie paid £1.9s.6d. tax for his four horses, and on Ainslie's 1821 map of Ayrshire (misspelled) as Tordoors. In the 1820s James Allison (1799-1879), from Lanarkshire's Avondale, bought the farm and, later in that decade, built the cottage – the two storey extension to the right is a later addition. The 1841 census shows it occupied by Robert Jack, a farm servant from Douglas, Lanarkshire, with his wife Grace and their four children. However, when Allison's 21 year old daughter Elizabeth married Doctor John Pearson (then 27 years old) of Newton Stewart in 1855, it became their home, until Pearson's death, from consumption, in May 1862. Their daughter, Elizabeth Allison Pearson died, unmarried, in the house in 1954, aged 96 years. Having come through Muirkirk's industrial period, the house now stands in a landscape of fields and woodland.

Crookedholm House, Crookedholm.

At the head of a winding driveway, on the north side of Crookedholm's Main Road (adjacent to what is now (2017) East Ayrshire Council's Crookedholm Depot), Crookedholm House appears on the 1856 Ordnance Survey map (published 1860), but it is not known who built, or first occupied, it. Its accommodation consisted of a drawing room, dining room, five bedrooms, four servants' bedrooms, wine and beer cellars, 'an excellent billiard room' and a coachman's house. From the early 1860s it was home to William Weir (1835-1913), the iron and coalmaster of the Portland Iron Company (Hurlford) and a partner in Messrs. William Baird & Company (he was a nephew to William Baird), who moved to Adamton House, Monkton in the early 1880s, where he died in September 1913, aged 78 years. The valuation roll for 1892-93 gives the owner as The Dowager Lady Howard de Walden, and the occupant as James Baird Thorneycroft (1851-1918), ironmaster. There followed a succession of tenants, including a stockbroker (Mr. Keir Cooper of London) and three or four Sheriff-Substitutes of Kilmarnock before falling into disrepair and ruin – aided by a fire. It is remembered as 'the sheriff's house' but was demolished in the 1970s and replaced by a new house which, following recent renovation, has been named 'Sheriff's Cottage'. The photograph was taken in the 1920s by Thomas Richardson Abbott, sub-postmaster, of Blair Avenue, Hurlford, who drowned in the River Irvine, near Ralstonyards Farm, in December 1936, aged 52 years.

Daldorch House (Catrine Bank), Catrine

Around 1820 Archibald Buchanan, manager of the Catrine Cotton Works, had Catrine Bank house built between the Sorn road and a sweeping bend in the river Ayr, for himself and his second wife, Hannah Struthers – a later extension, on the right, appears on the 1856 Ordnance Survey map, and brought the accommodation up to nine bedrooms. At his death in February 1841, Hannah was granted life-rental on the property, where she lived until her death in October 1856. Both were interred within a mausoleum in Sorn Churchyard, with their daughters; Agnes (1820-1838) and Margaret (1814-1839), wife of George Bogle of Rosemount. In February 1857 the 317 acre property, comprising of the house, and the farms Daldorch, Townhead and Shaw-Wood was let to Robert Thomson Pattison, whose connection with Catrine Mill is shown by the granting of a patent in December 1859 for *improvements in printing and dyeing certain woven fabrics and yarns*. The house was bought at auction in Glasgow by the Somervilles of Sorn Castle for £13,710, and remained with them until 1901 (on the bankruptcy of James Somervell) when it was bought by the ship and insurance broker John McKnight Campbell (1837-1906) of Glasgow – the estate name was carried by one of his ships, the SS *Daldorch*, launched by Scotts of Greenock in 1907 and torpedoed off Falmouth (as SS *Spital*) in January 1918. His son, William Hobart Campbell, died at the house in May 1945. It was later occupied by Teen Missions (Europe) Ltd. (a Christian missionary organisation, founded in 1978, but now dissolved) – which left it a little less tidy than when they arrived. Bought by the London-based Daldorch Estates Ltd, it was leased to the National Autism Society and converted to a residential school for autistic children, opened by the Princess Royal in May 1999.

Dean Castle, Kilmarnock

Dean Castle (once Kilmarnock Castle), with its Dower House, Keep and Palace, stands on the west bank of the Kilmarnock Water, north of the town. Central in this early 20th century photograph is the rectangular Keep, attributed to Sir Thomas Boyd (d.1350), but enlarged by a descendant, Robert Boyd, 1st Lord Boyd (d.1482), who built the palace (to the right) in the 1460s. Generations of the Boyd family occupied the estate until a serious fire in 1735 forced out William, the 4th Earl of Kilmarnock, who had built Kilmarnock House – but ended his days on London's Tower Hill for his part in the Jacobite Rebellion of 1745-46. Through marriage, the lands came to the 4th Duke of Portland and hence to the de Walden family. The Dower House dates from the mid 19th century. Between 1910 and 1946, the 8th Lord Howard de Walden carried through an extensive programme of restoration, including re-roofing both the Keep and the Palace. In 1975 John Osmael Scott-Ellis, 9th Lord Howard de Walden, gifted the estate to Kilmarnock and Loudoun District Council and it is now in the care of East Ayrshire Council.

The south-facing Dower House.

Taking for his model the 1584-87 built entry to Tolquhon Castle, Pitmedden, Aberdeenshire, the Edinburgh architect James Smith Richardson (1883-1970) designed this gatehouse for the 8th Baron, using stone from the demolished Kilmarnock House in St. Marnock Street. The topmost panel, above the arch, bears the de Walden coat of arms, with their motto; *Non Qvo Sed Qvomodo* (Not by whom, but in what manner) – *In Tenebris Lvx* (Light in darkness). The lower panel is inscribed – *This Warke* (work) *Wes Biggit* (built) *in 1936-37 on the Place Qvhair* (where) *the Foirentrie* (front entry) *Stood of Auld*. Rowallan Castle has been credited as the inspiration for the design, but the distinctive shot holes in the upper and lower floors and the sculpted panels, point firmly to Tolquhon.

Born on 9th May 1880, Thomas Evelyn Ellis (he changed his surname to Scott-Ellis in 1917) succeeded to the family's estates, as 8th Baron Howard de Walden (and 4th Baron Seaford), on the death of his father, Frederick George Ellis, in 1899 whilst a cadet at the Royal Military Academy, Sandhurst. A Lieutenant with the 10th Hussars in the Boer War, he served in the First World War as a Staff Captain, and Brevet Lieutenant-Colonel with the Royal Tank Corps. In February 1912 he married Margherita van Raalte (1890-1974) at St. Marylebone Parish Church, London. A patron of the arts, his many talents included oil painting, fiction writing and playwriting, whilst managing a vast estate around London's Oxford Street, Marylebone Road, Harley Street – and Dean Estate, which came to him through the female line from his great-grandmother, Henrietta Scott, wife of the 4th Duke of Portland. Between 1912 and 1946 the de Waldens lived (as tenants) at Chirk Castle in Denbighshire, with Dean Estate as their 'holiday home', despite the money he was spending on renovation work. When the lease on Chirk expired in March 1946, Dean Estate was their home until the Baron's death, in London, on 5th November that year. Despite his strong links to Wales, and his support for its culture, he chose Scotland as his final resting place. Following a memorial service in Kilmarnock's Laigh Kirk he was buried in the family crypt at Dean.

Reporting this garden party at Dean Castle, hosted by Lord Howard de Walden, on Saturday, 4th October 1913, the *Kilmarnock Standard* noted the town's 'society', *in countless little groups, star-scattered o'er the grass* fronting the Dower House. The first of many such gatherings was in January 1910 when, on first taking up residence, his Lordship entertained the workers and tradesmen responsible for the initial renovations.

Dollars House (Auchenskeith House), Riccarton

The initials 'C S' on this photograph of Dollars House suggests it to be the work of the Kilmarnock photographer Charles Semple – until 1855, a fruiterer and confectioner in the town's Waterloo Street – who, in the late 1850s, toured Ayrshire, photographing its houses and owners. Dollars estate was then owned by the Honourable Mrs. Jean Macadam Cathcart of Craigengillan and occupied by Lady Adelaide Hastings. Blaeu's 1654 Atlas of Scotland has it as a fortalice named 'Dullers', but it is a house on Armstrong's 1775 map of Ayrshire. Taylor & Skinner's map of 1776, shows *Auchenskeigh, Capt. Cunningham Esq.*, and John Thomson's 1832 map has it as 'Dallars'. The early history of the property is lost, other than the name Archibald Dunlop, who married an unnamed daughter of Craufurdland. The first Cunningham of Dullers may have been William (d.1760s), grandfather of the *Capt Cunningham* of Taylor and Skinner's map. He is listed in the Servants Tax Roll for 1777-78, for Auchenskeith, as having one servant, John Begbie, and was probably responsible for transforming the fortalice to a house. By 1803 Quintin Macadam (b.1769) of Berbeth, Straiton was the new owner, and on his death, by suicide (1805), Sir William Cunningham, was a trustee of his estate. After years of rental, it was home to Honoria Mary, daughter of Colonel William Macadam, when she married Edward Carleton Tufnell (1806-1886) in 1847. Eton and Balliol College educated, Tufnell was a commissioner of the Poor Laws in London from 1835 until 1846 and a force in setting up teacher training colleges. The family name lives on with the London area of Tufnell, and the underground station Tufnell Park. They were succeeded by their son, Commander Carleton Tufnell (1848-1893) of the Royal Navy. In 1962 the property was bought by the Richards family, and much-needed renovation work carried out.

The rear quarters of the house.

Drongan House

Drongan House, on the south side of the Ayr to Cumnock road at Coalhall, in the early 1920s when, as a farmhouse, it was owned by David Downie, a merchant, and occupied by his brother-in-law James Lymburn. The mansion house was built in 1776 by Mungo Smith (1738-1814), incorporating the previous house Lochmark (the crow-stepped gable to the right) and accessed from today's Coalhall to Drongan road – two surviving lines of trees mark the driveway from the west. The property's future value was in the two seam coalfield below it; one of three feet thick at 162 feet and the other ten feet thick at 222 feet. Smith's nineteen year old son, and heir, John, joined the bankers, Fergusson & Co. in Calcutta in 1805, and during a return visit to Drongan in 1819, had plans drawn to improve the house. However, he died of cholera, at Calcutta, in 1830 aged 44 years. By 1855 the estate was in the hands of Alexander Oswald of Auchincruive but his interest was in the coal and not the house, which he left to deteriorate. In January 1869 Auchincruive's youngest daughter, Edith Mary, married Captain John Manners Yorke of the Royal Navy (1840-1909) at St. George's Church, Hanover Square, London. Yorke became 'lord of the manor' – his name appearing on the Valuation Roll – but never resided in the house. It was later renovated and improved, and survives as a farmhouse.

Dumfries House, Cumnock

The contract between William Crichton-Dalrymple (1699-1768), 5th Earl of Dumfries, and the architect brothers Adam – John (1721-1792), Robert (1728-1792) and James (1732-1794) – to build Dumfries House, was signed on 16th May 1754. The initial (1751) estimate for the work (including offices and drains) was £9,182.10s.9d., but reduced to £7,979.11s.2d. at the fourth, and final, estimate. Drawings for the Palladian style villa had been made by the architects' father, William Adam (1689-1748) in the 1740s, but reworked, principally, by John. At this period the brothers were also working on Hopetoun House, Linlithgow (1750-1754), Yester House, Gifford (1758-1761) and Arniston House, Midlothian (1754-1758). The foundation stone was laid on 18th July 1754, and the first instalment, of £1,500, paid the following week. The estate remained with the Dumfries family until 2004, when the 27th Earl of Dumfries, 'Johnnie Dumfries' decided to sell it, hopefully to the National Trust for Scotland, and send the most valuable of its contents to auction. At the last minute it was saved by the intervention of the Prince

of Wales and now (2017), under the management of the Great Steward of Scotland's Dumfries House Trust, is an increasingly important visitor attraction.

Built in 1760, at a cost of £279.17s.7d., the Temple Gateway would straddle the main (as yet unbuilt) driveway from Barony Road, south, to the Avenue Bridge, as the estate's main entrance – the entry from the Ayr / Cumnock road to be the 'trades entrance'. Unfortunately, the Temple, with its lodges, stood on the Dumfries and Auchinleck estates boundary, and as an afterthought, Lord Auchinleck's permission to build the road across his land was sought – and refused. The lodges on either side housed estate workers, but over the years were abandoned. They were restored in 2016.

Bridge at Dumfries House, Cumnock

Costing £430.16s.2d., the Avenue Bridge was to carry the main driveway from the Temple Gateway over the River Lugar, to the house. Its three semi-elliptical arch design is attributed to John Adam and bears similarities to the architect Robert Morris's Garron Bridge at Inveraray Castle (1747), where Adam had also been employed. A 1754 drawing shows the obelisks added in pencil, their addition, perhaps, influenced by Robert Adam's 1755 visit to Rome, where there were more Egyptian obelisks than remained in the land of the Pharaohs.

John Patrick Crichton-Stuart, 3rd Marquess of Bute, was born at Mount Stuart House, Bute on 12th September 1847, the only child of John Crichton-Stuart, the 2nd Marquess (1793-1848) and Sophia Frederica Christina (b.1809) – becoming a ward in chancery on the death of his mother in 1859. Educated at Harrow School, Middlesex and Christ College, Oxford, where he studied religion, he was received into the Roman Catholic Church at the chapel of the Sisters of Notre Dame, Southwark, London in 1868 – causing something of a sensation. On coming of age and gaining control of the family's extensive estates in Scotland and Wales, he completed Cardiff Docks, work started by his father, and served two terms as the city's mayor in the 1890s. He is commemorated by a statue in Cardiff's

Friary Gardens, opposite Bute Park. His munificence to places of learning brought a Chair of Anatomy, a medical hall and a students' union hall to St. Andrews University, and the completion of Bute Hall at Glasgow University. A patron of architecture, he rebuilt Cardiff Castle and, after a fire in 1877, Mount Stuart House on Bute. He died at Dumfries House on 9th October 1900 from an apoplectic attack aged 53 years. The Statue of the Crucifixion in Shaw Wood, to the north-east of the house, at the confluence of the Rose Burn and the Lugar Water, was raised to his memory. At its top are the letters 'INRI' – *Iesus Nazerenus Rex Iudaeorum* (Jesus of Nazareth, King of the Jews) – whilst on the shaft, are the words, *Thy wounds are my merits*, attributed to the Cistercian abbot, Bernard of Clairvaux (1090-1153). On Friday, 12th October 1900 the Marquess was buried in the chapel at his Mount Stuart estate on Bute. Within hours of death, his heart was removed, sealed in a heart-shaped glass vessel and placed within a heart-shaped casket for burial in Jerusalem, where he had bought a house in 1880. On 13th November 1900 the casket was interred in the grounds of the Dominus Flevit (the Lord wept) Chapel on the Mount of Olives, with a small, but ornate, iron cross over it. The Latin inscription on the base of the Dumfries House memorial reads; *HAEC SACROSANCTA IMAGO JUSSU JOANNIS MARCHIONIS III BOTHAE ERECTA EST PROPE LOCUM UBI IPSE ANIMAM DEO REDDIDIT IX OCTOBR ANN MDCCCC* – 'This sacred image was erected on the wishes of John, the 3rd Marquess of Bute near to the place where his spirit returned to God on 9th October 1900'.

On Thursday, 6th July 1905, the 4th Marquis of Bute, John Crichton-Stuart (1881-1947), married Augusta Mary Monica Bellingham, the 25 year old daughter of Sir Henry Bellingham of Castlebellingham in Co. Louth, Ireland. The marriage was celebrated at the Bute estates at Cardiff and Dumfries House, on the Saturday, when this photograph was taken. Some 500 schoolchildren from Cumnock, New Cumnock, Auchinleck and Ochiltree, with their teachers, were invited to a grand fete in the field opposite the estate's main entrance. There, a liberal supply of milk and buns, 'amusements of many kinds' – including the swings pictured – and entertainment was provided by brass and pipe bands. Unlike those at Cardiff, the Ayrshire children were not presented with commemorative mugs – but the weather was better.

Dunlop House, Dunlop

Writing the *Statistical Account* for Dunlop Parish in January 1836, the Rev. Matthew Dickie records that – *Dunlop House is another relic of former times, which has now disappeared. It was taken down about three years ago to make way for a splendid new mansion.* For his new house, Sir John Dunlop, MP for Ayrshire (1833-1839), commissioned the Glasgow architect David Hamilton (1768-1843). A door lintel, bearing the dates 1599 and 1601, was retained from the old and incorporated into the new. Hamilton was the maternal grandfather of Madeleine Hamilton Smith of Blythswood Square, Glasgow. Born in 1835, she was tried at the High Court at Edinburgh in 1857 for the murder, by arsenic poisoning, of her lover Pierre Emile L'Angelier. The jury returned a verdict of Not Proven. Sir John Dunlop was created a baronet on the ascension of Queen Victoria in 1838, but died at Hastings the following year, aged 34, leaving a widow, Lady Harriet Primrose, eldest daughter of the Earl of Rosebery. When his son, Major Sir James Dunlop of the Coldstream Guards died, unmarried, in the south of France in 1858, the baronetage became extinct, and the estate was bought by a cousin, Thomas Dunlop Douglas, and passed through a number of owners and tenants. This photograph was used in Millar's book *The Castles and Mansions of Ayrshire*.

Convalescing servicemen, with their Voluntary Aid Detachment nurses, at the rear stairway of Dunlop House during the First World War when, thanks to Mrs. Eleanor Louisa Houison Craufurd, it was an auxiliary hospital. In 1933 Ayr County Council bought the estate for an orphanage, then a 72 bed mental hospital, under the management of Glengall Asylum (now Ailsa Hospital), Ayr. In 1992 it was owned by Radio Frequency Investigation Ltd (dissolved 2008) as an electronics laboratory, until bought in, or around, 2003 for development and conversion to ten flatted dwellings, with houses in the grounds.

The bridge over the Clerkland Burn, a tributary of the River Irvine, around 1905, which carried the driveway to the stables, and is contemporary with the house. The left bank is in Stewarton Parish and the right in Dunlop. In autumn 2001, whilst the developer, it is said, was clearing debris from under the already fragile bridge, it collapsed but, under a planning enforcement order, was re-built using synthetic stone, the original material having been removed from the site.

The conservatory against the north-west wall of the walled garden with the gardener at its doorway.

The estate's West Lodge, on the Dunlop to Neilston road, is contemporary with the house, but was enlarged in 1905. It has survived, as has the crescent of spear-headed cast iron railing, although the gates and the centre pillars have been removed.

East Halket House, Dunlop

The family of John Boyle Kerr (1822-1901) at the south-facing front of East Halket House in the 1890s. A native of Stewarton, Kerr took the tenancy of the 115 acre farm around 1860, with his wife Isabella and their children, Hugh (b.1854) and Maggie (b.1858). A further four children were born here – James (b.1861), Robert (b.1864), Isabella (b.1866) and Janet (b.1868). Kerr's landlord, to whom he paid £170 per annum, was Alexander Wylie (1792-1869) who, in 1847, converted the farmhouse to this modest country house, adding a second storey and bringing the entry from the rear to the front and giving it a Doric pillared portico. The Ordnance Survey Name Book (1855-1857) describes the house as; *A good arable farmsteading – perhaps the best in the parish.*

Elmbank House, Kilmarnock

On the south side of London Road, James Gregg, Kilmarnock's Town Clerk had Elmbank House built around 1792, naming it Lewisville (or Louisville) for his wife Lewis Brown whom he had married in 1790. Gregg died in 1818 'in an advanced age' and the property was sold to the family of Patrick Clark of Holms, Galston, a merchant, who had passed away in 1796. John Wood's 1819 map shows the house as *Elmwood Bank, 'occupied by Mrs. Clarke'.*

The last of the Clark family, Janet Elizabeth, died in February 1873, aged 86 years, and the house was bought by the coalmaster John Gilmour. In his early life, Gilmour had been a driver with the Glasgow and South Western Railway but, *was an instance, not uncommon here, of a self-made man rising to a position of considerable importance.* He gifted £350 for a new organ in St. Marnock's Church (1872) and laid the foundation stone of the Operetta House in Kilmarnock's John Finnie Street in 1874 (East Ayrshire Council offices from 2013). Heavy losses in mining speculations brought bankruptcy and he died in January 1891, aged 73, at Hillhead, Coylton. Kilmarnock Town Council bought Elmbank and its grounds in 1893 to house its public library, then in the Corn Exchange Buildings in Green Street, and it was opened in February 1895 by Sheriff Substitute David Hall of Crookedholm House. This was recognised as a stop-gap, and in May 1897, James Dick (1823-1902), a native of Kilmarnock, but then, with his brother Robert, a gutta percha manufacturer in Glasgow signed a Deed of Gift – '… *being desirous to do something for Kilmarnock, my native town, I hereby agree and oblige myself to erect and gift to Kilmarnock a new building at a cost not exceeding eight thousand pounds, to be used as the Public Library and Museum, and to be erected on the site of Elmbank House …*'. The foundation stone of the Dick Institute was laid on 17th September 1898 and opened in April 1901, leaving the name Elmbank to the streets around it.

Garrallan House, Cumnock

A family group outside the north-east facing front of Garrallan House. To the right the driveway sweeps down to the Skares road after bridging the Rose Burn. The individuals in the photograph cannot be named. In 1562 Hew Campbell (d.1602) obtained a charter for the lands of Garrallan from Sir Matthew Campbell of Loudoun which, by the 1880s, extended to 594 acres, including the house and its policies, Changue Farm, the smithy and woodland. In 1648 Hew Campbell's grand-daughter Margaret married George Douglas of Waterside (an estate north-west of Dumfries Estate), the titles passing to their son, Hugh, in 1676. The last 'Douglas' was Dr. Patrick Douglas, who died of frailty in November 1819, aged 91 years, and appears in the 1785 Horse Tax Roll, paying 10/- tax for a horse. His daughter, Jane Douglas, had married Hamilton Boswell of Knockroon, a solicitor and Collector of Taxes for Ayrshire, at Ayr in March 1807, and being his only child, succeeded. Excepting the removal of the chimney on the left, the house looks much the same today. The entrance porch was added by John Douglas Boswell (1812-1863), son of Hamilton Boswell, in 1856, and the four chimney pot topped extension to the right was built for Patrick Charles Douglas Boswell in 1868. With the death of Patrick and Annabella's son, John Douglas Boswell in 1948, aged 80 years, the house was sold to the Stevenson family, tenants of Changue Farm.

The stone, HD + MC 1676, set into one of two south-facing gables, celebrates the marriage of Hugh Douglas (1648-1719) to Margaret Craufurd in 1676. He was the son of Margaret Campbell of Garrallane, who had married George Douglas of Waterside and succeeded to the estate in 1648, whilst Margaret was the only daughter of John Craufurd of Camlarg. Their eldest son, John Douglas, died c.1699 in Panama, playing his part in the Darien venture – the failed Scottish attempt to establish a colony on the Isthmus of Panama – leaving the succession to their second born, Hugh, in 1719. His son, Patrick, followed in 1776 and his grand-daughter, Jane in 1819.

The adjacent south gable also holds a celebration stone – PCDB – AACI – 1874, for Patrick Charles Douglas Boswell (b.1815) and Annabella Alexandrina Campbell Innes (b.1826). The fifth child of Hamilton Boswell and Jane Douglas, Charles emigrated to Australia where, in 1849, he met Annabella, the daughter of George Innes, a landholder, whilst manager of the Bank of New South Wales at Newcastle. They married in June 1856 and returned to Garrallan, with their four children, in 1865 when Patrick inherited the estate on the death of his elder brother, John Douglas Boswell. Patrick died in September 1892 and Annabella in October 1914.

Gilmilnscroft, Sorn

The name Farquhar was associated with the Gilmilnscroft estate from the 14th century – '*anno 1407, an infeftment* (investing with legal possession) *was granted by Agnes Wallace, gudewife of Gilmilnscroft, and relict of Robert Farquhar, to her son, Alexander Farquhar*' – and continued, through branches of the family in Ayrshire and Aberdeenshire. The last of the Ayrshire family, Miss Jane Gray Farquhar died in March 1884, the estate passing to her nearest kin, Sir Henry Farquhar of Mounie in Aberdeenshire, who moved to Gilmilnscroft. He died in January 1916, in his 78th year, and the estate was managed by trustees. In the early 1960s it was a boarding school, offering 'character formation and a good general education', but is now in private hands.

This 1903/04 photograph shows the original avenue into Gilmilnscroft, opposite Barrshouse steading, from the minor road to the north-west of the house, which runs parallel to the Sorn–Catrine road. The avenue and its trees appear on the 1856 Ordnance Survey map. The surface is not rutted, suggesting it was little used after the building of the driveway from the main road at the gatehouse. As a footnote, Lewis Stenning is of interest. Born at Sorn in 1901 he started his working life as a gardener at Gilmilnscroft and in 1924 was a student gardener at Kew Gardens, London where, from 1960 until his death in 1965 he was the garden's curator.

Girgenti, Stewarton

The south-facing front of Girgenti on a summer's day in the early 1880s, when owned by Alexander Cochrane of the Verreville pottery in Glasgow's Finnieston Street. Standing on the north of the road from Cunninghamhead to Torranyard, it was built in the late 1820s by Captain John Cheape, who bought 55 acres of land from Thomas Reid of Stacklawhill in 1827 for £1,350. It is not known who designed the house, who built it, or why Cheape named it Girgenti (had he visited Malta or Sicily?). Writing the *Statistical Account* for Stewarton, in January 1842, the Rev. Charles Bannatyne Steven noted the modern buildings in his parish, and their owners – Mr. Cunninghame of Lainshaw, Mr. Kerr of Robertland, Colonel S. M'Alister of Kennox and Captain Cheape of Girgenti – *This last is built in rather an uncommon style*. The gatehouses at its two entries survive, as do the walls of the garden adjacent to the west gatehouse. The 1841 census gives Cheape's occupation as 'Captain in the Army'. In the *London Gazette*, of 25th July 1795, he appears as an ensign with the 44th Regiment of Foot, transferring (by purchase) to the 98th Regiment and, in the August, to the Royal Glasgow Regiment of Foot, as a captain. In February 1800, he joined the 3rd Regiment of Foot Guards (from 1831-1877 – The Scots Fusilier Guards and from 1877 the Scots Guards) as a lieutenant until 1803, when he retired with the rank of captain. As evidence of his interest in farming, he was presented with an honorary silver medal by the Royal Horticultural and Agricultural Society of Scotland for his report on *Cultivation of Land by Manual Labour*, published in 1833.

Cheape never married and died in the house on 10th February 1850 leaving the estate administration to his near neighbour, James M'Alister of Kennox. In his last will, dated 9th August 1847, life-rent of the estate passed to his sister Marianna, wife of Thomas Bowes-Lyon, 11th Earl of Strathmore, but as she had died in October 1849 the estate was sold and the proceeds divided amongst the infirmaries at Glasgow, Edinburgh, Inverness, Aberdeen and Dumfries, each receiving approximately £1,800. A codicil in this last will reads; *having good reason to be dissatisfied with the conduct of Euphemia McKinnon, I hereby revoke the legacy to her of £50*. He lies under a large sandstone obelisk in the grounds of Stewarton's St. Columba's Parish Church. The advertisement for the auction

sale of the house (upset price £3,800), within the King's Arms Inn, Irvine, in October 1851, details its accommodation: four public rooms, eight bedrooms (six with dressing closets), and a conservatory, besides a sunk storey containing eight rooms, affording ample accommodation for servants. There was also a double coach house and stable (the current house), barn, byre and milk-house etc.

An early 20th century photograph of Girgenti's, eight sided, 80 feet high tower viewed from the north with the coach house and stables to the right. Its pinnacle came down, intact, in a storm some years ago. In addition to its four clock faces, it has a raised sandstone shield-shaped plaque on its east face inscribed – *Designed and Erected by Captain John Cheape MDCCCXLIII [1843]* – and on the south face a crest, with a sheaf of corn, above the motto *DITAT VITTUS* – 'virtue enriches' – and a shield with three ears of corn. This comes from the Cheape family of Rossie in Fife, his family and forebearers. Despite the motto's clear lettering it has, over the years, been read as *DIDAT FRUCTUS* – 'let it spread its fruit abroad'. As to why Cheape built the tower, theories abound. One has him a smuggler (possibly true had he been a sea captain and not an army captain) and the tower a means of signalling to contraband ships in the Firth, whilst in another he was a Re-incarnationist who would return as a dove – successive owners having the responsibility of leaving his food at the top of the tower. A more mundane reason may be deduced from the date – 1846. The record of his birth and baptism is lost, but the 1841 census gives his age as 67 years, hence, give or take a year, the tower may have been in celebration of his 70th year.

Glaisnock House, Cumnock

In his *General Report of the Agricultural State and Political Circumstances of Scotland*, published in 1813, Sir John Sinclair of Ulbster – who was responsible for the 21 volume *Statistical Account of Scotland* of the 1790s – wrote that Alexander Allason bought the 895 acre Glaisnock estate in 1791 and by ploughing, delving and liming, converted its moorland into arable land, before dividing it into six farms. In 1835 Allason, and his brother James, commissioned the Kilmarnock architect James Ingram to design and supervise the building of a new house in Tudor Manorial style – Ingram's first major commission. The initial build stands to the left in this late 19th century photograph, facing north-east. The original house became the stable and coach house. On James Allason's death in 1850, aged 93 years, the estate passed to Richard Bannatine, whose mother Jean Allason (b. 1780) was the daughter of Robert Allason of Cowdam (later Coodham), and niece of Glaisnock, who had married Richard Bannatine of Edinburgh, at Symington in March 1805. The estate passed to the Bannatines' son, Richard Cunningham Allason Bannatine, who died at Tunbridge, Kent in October 1867. By the turn of the century, it was owned by Capt. Robert Mitchell Campbell of Auchmannoch and Avisyard. Ayr County Council bought it in 1949, and between September 1952 and 1973 it was a school under the charge of John Weir, DSO, OBE, JP, MA, FEIS, (1913-2005) with, at times, up to 135 pupils, some of whom were boarders. It has also been an 'outdoor centre' and an arts centre under the Glaisnock Trust. By 2015, whilst undergoing renovation, the ivy was removed, as was the conservatory on the right and the mature tree on the left.

James Ingram, architect, Kilmarnock. Born on 15th August 1799 in Dalgain Street, Sorn, where his father, Andrew, was a wright, James Ingram would have started his schooling in the village, but nothing is known of his later education or architectural training. His first commission appears to have been the Martyr's Parish Church, New Cumnock in 1831, followed by buildings in Kilmarnock's King Street and St. Marnock's Parish Church on St. Marnock Street in 1834. The following year brought the commission for Glaisnock House. In 1846 he worked from Guard Street (off King Street), Kilmarnock, and in 1850 from Portland Terrace and, finally, an office at 114 King Street from 1868. He married Mary Sampson at Sorn in 1828 and two of their sons, William (b.1835) and Robert (b.1841), joined the business – with a branch in Glasgow's West Regent Street. He died, a widower, at 41 Dundonald Road, Kilmarnock in July 1879.

Glenbuck House, Glenbuck

Overlooking Glenbuck Loch – one of two reservoirs on the River Ayr which supplied the cotton works at Catrine – the Scottish Baronial style Glenbuck House was built in 1879 for Charles Howatson of Dornel and Glenbuck by Boyd & Forrest of Kilmarnock and Stewarton, to plans by the architect John Murdoch of Ayr (1825-1907). Howatson came from farming stock in the Auchinleck–Cronberry area, but deserted the land, as a 15 year old around 1847, to work for the ironfounder Wm. Baird & Co. at Gartsherrie in Lanarkshire – their purchase of the Glenbuck Iron Works in the 1850s bringing Howatson back to Ayrshire, as foundry manager. Prior to his retiral in 1870, he had been buying farms – Dornel, Hall, Glenmuir, Auchinlongford and, finally, Glenbuck (then a farm) in 1872. His investment in the draining and improvement of these farms won him international recognition as a breeder of black faced sheep. In 1859, as a 26 year old, he had married Wilhelmina Aird Fletcher (d.1887), the 32 year old daughter of Angus Fletcher of Crossflatt. Howatson was also interested in what lay beneath the grass his sheep grazed on, opening mines to extract the gas-rich coal. He died at the house in January 1918. Its relatively short life ended with its demolition in the summer of 1948, when a proposal to convert it to flatted accommodation proved too costly.

Gowanbank House, Darvel.

The Weekly Advertiser for Galston, Newmilns and Darvel of 11th September 1880 reported; GOWANBANK VILLA – *We have almost seen the completion of this beautiful villa, which is being erected for Messrs. A & R Morton, of the firm of Alex. Morton & Co. The building, in itself, far surpasses anything of a similar nature in the district, Lanfine Manor not even being worthy of comparison with it.* Neither the architect nor the builder are known but the money came from the successful lace business of Alexander Morton. Born in 1844, Morton's entrepreneurial skills transformed weaving from a cottage industry, working for Glasgow-based agents, to an industrial scale employing hundreds in the Irvine Valley. In the spring of 1881 he and his family moved to Gowanbank from Ranoldcoup Road, Darvel. *The Weekly Advertiser* also observed; *… it shows to all who pass by that way, and in a very forcible manner, what may be*

attained by a sober, diligent, and intelligent perseverance in the path of business duties. Morton established a stud farm on the rising ground behind the house, with annual sales of hackneys and ponies at which, in 1893, 65 animals passed under the hammer for £3,872. He was a member of Darvel Parish Council and chairman of the school board. He died at his fruit farm, Bruckless House, in County Donegal on 28th December 1923 and was interred at Darvel on New Year's Day 1924. A public subscription memorial to him, by the sculptor Sir Robert Lorimer, was erected at the roadside below Gowanbank in 1926. By the 1970s the house was a hotel, with a resident band, *Just Three*, who in 1974 produced an LP record, *Saturday Night at Gowanbank*. The hotel was lost to a fire in January 1982 but, rebuilt, is once again (2017) offering bed and breakfast accommodation.

Hallhouse, Fenwick

The original farmhouse style Hallhouse, in Laigh Fenwick, dates from the late 18th century when its entrance was opposite Waterslap. It was built for Robert Sawer, a surgeon, who later added the present two storey Georgian style front, with its fluted Doric columned entry, shortly before his death in March 1832, aged 71 years, and burial in Fenwick Churchyard. Ownership passed to his daughter Mary (1798-1869) and her husband James Thomson (1801-1861), an English-born Professor of Dancing whom she had married in Kilmarnock's Laigh Kirk in March 1826. Over the years owners came and went, leading to today's Hillhouse Care Home, but in February 1886 an action in the Court of Session made news. Thomas Walker of Pittsburgh, Pennsylvania, USA, on behalf of his sister Mrs. Margaret Walker or Howat, claimed that Alexander Cunningham had taken possession of Hillhouse illegally, the rightful owners being the Walker family. The 1881 census for Fenwick shows 46 year old, Saltcoats born, Cunningham, whose income came from dealing in land and houses, living at Hallhouse with his wife Maggie and his mother Eliza. The 1885 Valuation Roll shows him as proprietor of Hallhouse, and 98 Commerce Street, Glasgow. The court found in Walker's favour, and the title deeds were corrected, and damages and expenses, assessed at £25, paid by Cunningham. In 2017 Hallhouse was a care home.

Hareshaw Lodge, Fenwick

In December 1886 the 6th Earl of Glasgow, George Boyle (1825-1890), had his Fenwick Estate – some 10,000 acres divided into seven lots – auctioned at the George Hotel, Kilmarnock. Lot G, extending to 5,043 acres, comprised ten farms, a shooting lodge (Hareshaw Lodge, built in the 1870s) and one of the best grouse moors in Ayrshire, yielding 283 brace of grouse in two days, and was bought by 30 year old George Colvin White of Dankeith and Stewartlea, Ayr, at the upset price of £32,000. On his marriage certificate of 1882, White gave his occupation as 'Railway Shareholder', but later disappeared in a cloud of bankruptcy. In 1894 he sold the estate, for £38,000, to the Glasgow cotton merchant, Andrew Brown Paton (1833-1913), a descendant of the Covenanter, Captain John Paton (executed at Edinburgh on 9th May 1684), who was born at Meadowhead Farm, now part of his descendant's property. Andrew retired in August 1889 and moved to Hareshaw Lodge, adding a number of extensions. He was succeeded by his nephew, Edward Richmond Paton, whose book, *The Birds of Hareshawmuir*, was published by the *Kilmarnock Standard* in 1925, and who died in the house in 1957.

An Edwardian period photograph of the house with, perhaps, Andrew Paton in the carriage.

Built to house the estate's gamekeeper, William Fingland and his family, the cottage dates from the 1870s. Born at Closeburn, Dumfriesshire in 1841, Fingland had lived in Waterside village with his Stewarton-born wife, Jeannie (*née* Highet), and the first of their six children, Charles. As the lodge was rented to tenants during the shooting season, William and Jeannie would have played host to many visitors. He died at the cottage in January 1927 in his 86th year.

Hillhouse Lodge, Fenwick

Standing east of Craufurdland Water and north of the road to High Grassyards Farm, Hillhouse Lodge, shown here around 1904, appears on Captain Andrew Armstrong & Son's New Map of Ayrshire, published in 1775, as Hillhouse. John White, huntsman to the Gentlemen of Kilmarnock Hunt, lived here in 1797 paying 5/- tax for each of the hunt's 32 dogs. *The Glasgow Herald* of 20th July 1827 carried an advertisement for the sale of the property … *The cottage contains Dining-room, Drawing-room, Library, and six bedrooms with stable and other out-houses. The Garden and Orchard are well stocked with Fruit Trees … . The Property extends to 48 Scotch Acres* (61 Imperial acres) *of Arable Land, and has a good steading of Farm-houses. The Cottage, which would afford a delightful residence for anyone seeking retirement, may be sold either with the whole or only part of the Lands, as purchasers may incline.* It may have been bought by William Smith, shown as the occupier in *Pigot's Directory* of 1837, but by 1841 it was home to Alexander Picken, 'a gentleman of independent means', and his family. On his death in December 1846 the estate passed to his 39 year old son James Hunter Picken (d. 1879) who, in June that year, had married Jane Samson, the 38 year old daughter of the Kilmarnock nurseryman, Thomas Samson. Picken was a Justice of the Peace and further marked his position as a gentleman, by becoming captain of the 1st Company of the Ayrshire Rifle Volunteers in January 1860.

Hillside House, Cumnock

On his death at Causeyhead on Dumfries Estate, Cumnock in 1846, 73 year old Adam Crichton, factor to the Marquess of Bute's Ayrshire estates, bequeathed a number of properties and plots of land in, and around, Cumnock, to his son Hew (1794-1891), a Writer to the Signet and partner in the Edinburgh law firm Tait & Crichton. On one of these plots, Hangman's Acre, on the south side of Barrhill Road, he had Hillside House built as a summer retreat for his family. Hew Crichton died in Edinburgh on Thursday, 28th May 1891, aged 97 years. His son, James Arthur Crichton, died the following day, aged 66 years, and they were buried together, at Edinburgh's Dean Cemetery. James Arthur Crichton had been the Sheriff Principal of Lothians and Peebles, and had led the prosecution case against Dr. Edward William Pritchard, hanged at Glasgow in July 1865 for the murder of his wife and mother-in-law by poison. In memory of the father and son, the surviving son, Hew Hamilton Crichton (1820-1906), also a Writer to the Signet, and his sister Margaret Crichton funded the building of the Crichton Memorial Church, on Ayr Road, Cumnock. Margaret died at South Nelson Street, Edinburgh in March 1908 having made over Hillside House, and the Black Bull Hotel, to Andrew Forrester, Writer to the Signet. He sold the house to Cumnock School Board which converted it to school accommodation.

Hollybush House (Over Skeldon), Dalrymple

Cresting a rise above the north bank of the River Doon, east of Dalrymple, this new Hollybush House was built in 1855 for Frederick Andrew Eck, to plans by the Ayr-based architect Robert Paton – the following year Paton was working on the Union Bank of Scotland's building at 128 High Street, Ayr. The landscape and garden architect, Charles Hope Smith of Edinburgh, designed the grounds and, as the photograph is undated, the apparently new fencing may show his work (the stand of trees in the centre of the photograph survives). The 670 acre estate with its thatched, two storey, house (habitable until at least the 1890s) was bought by John Hunter

(1746-1823), Writer to the Signet (a senior solicitor to the Court of Session), of Doohholm, Ayr in 1797, changing its name from Over Skeldon to Hollybush, and is just visible to the right. Born at Vevey, on the north shore of Lake Geneva, Eck joined the London trading company Antony Gibbs and Sons as a 17 year old in 1823 and, with his gift for languages, was sent to Lima, Peru, from where Gibbs exported the manure, guano. By the 1840s he was in Valparaiso, in charge of Gibbs interests in Chile. In June 1846 at Glasgow, he married Janet Alexander, returning to South America, where the first two of their four children were born. The third, Blanche-Louisa was born in Edinburgh, as was William Frederick, their only son, with his birth also registered in Dalrymple Parish. Eck died in February 1884 at 100 Cromwell Road, Kensington, London (now the Crowne Plaza Hotel) and Hollybush was sold, in 1891, to the first of a succession of owners, Sir Claud Alexander of Ballochmyle.

The south-west facing rear of the house, looking to the River Doon.

A busy day at Hollybush House Hotel in the late 1940s or early 1950s when, 'The Most Beautiful Hotel in Ayrshire', offered the comforts of central heating, log fires, comfortable bedrooms, spacious lounges and a magnificent ballroom. Business waxed and waned as owners came and went until 1984 when it was bought by the Veterans' Mental Welfare Charity – Combat Stress.

Holmes House, Galston

The Tudor style Holmes House, on the rising ground south of the Hurlford to Galston road in the early 1880s, when owned and occupied by William Fairlie (1826-1893). On returning to this country in 1796, from a successful mercantile career in America's Maryland, his great uncle, Mungo Fairlie (1752-1819), bought the 12 acre Holmes estate and, entering local life, was appointed a deputy lieutenant of the county in 1803 and a captain of the Ayrshire Militia in 1808. He and his brother James of Bellfield (but late of Jamaica), Patrick Ballantine of Castlehill House, Ayr, George Douglas of Rodinghead and William Parker of Assloss founded the Kilmarnock Banking Company which traded from 1802 until 1821, when it was taken over by Hunter & Co. of Ayr. Mungo died unmarried and the estate passed to his nephew, James Fairlie of Bellfield (1794-1860). The form of the house occupied by Mungo is not known, James having built the house in the illustration, in the 1820s. Its accommodation consisted of four public rooms, thirteen bedrooms, staff quarters and outside offices providing stabling, coach houses, and harness room, with houses for a coachman and a groom. The 1841 census shows James, his 35 year old wife, Agnes, their eight children, and a staff of thirteen (one governess, two male servants and ten female servants). The last of the direct family was James, son of William, who died at Alderholt near Salisbury in June 1926, aged 46 years. By the early 1930s the house was unoccupied, and to reduce the rateable value from £100 to £50 the roof was removed and the north facing front taken down, leaving the remainder to the support of trees and ivy.

Kameshill House, Muirkirk

An early 20th century, winter's day, photograph of Kameshill (Kaimeshill) House when owned by William Baird & Co., the coal and iron masters and occupied, from 1870 until 1915 by the manager of their Muirkirk operations, John Angus and his family. The original house, perhaps known as 'High Hill', may have dated from 1700 and appears on Herman Moll's map of 1745 as 'Kems' and the Ordnance Survey map of 1856 as Kaimeshill. In a lecture to the Muirkirk Literary Association and Lapraik Burns Club in January 1927, Dugald Baird (1860-1947), who had succeeded John Angus as manager, said that from report books kept by managers at the works from March 1787, it was agreed in September, 1790, to build an addition to Kameshill House, and that the foundation was "stabbed off." William Gardiner dug it out, and John Paterson built it. Further additions were made between 1906 and 1911 to drawings by the architect David Morton Brown of Ingram & Brown, Kilmarnock. The iron works closed in 1921 and following the nationalisation of the coal industry in 1948 the condition of the unoccupied house became such that it was demolished in 1954.

The south-west rear quarter of the house in summer.

Kennox House, Stewarton

Straddling the Irvine road, two miles west of Stewarton, Kennox estate extended to 197 acres of arable land with grass parks, one farm and a number of cottages, with the south running Glazert Burn (once serving Crivoch Mill) to the east. The original house, extending to the left in this photograph, was built about 1720 by James Sommerville, who brought the name from the Douglas area of Lanarkshire. In March 1792 his grand-daughter, Jessie (or Janet) (1764-1852), married Charles M'Alister of Loup, a captain with the Sommerville Bank Company of the Argyllshire Volunteers, at Kilcalmonell in Argyllshire. When the volunteers disbanded in June 1802, *The Caledonian Mercury* newspaper reported that Captain M'Alister was leaving to reside in his newly acquired estate of Kennox in Ayrshire. M'Alister became chief of his Argyllshire clan, and took the name Charles Sommerville M'Alister, perhaps to strengthen his connection with Kennox. He was appointed a deputy-lieutenant of Ayrshire and for a time was commandant of the First Regiment of the Ayrshire Volunteers. He died in October 1847, in his 83rd year, having added the new 'front' to the house in the 1820s.

The rearmost part of the house in the 1890s, was in sharp contrast to the clean lines of its front.

A 24 pane window on the east side of the house bears two engravings – *Will Somervell* and *John Bell, August 10, 1740*. If the engravings are contemporaneous, this was three years before William Somerville succeeded to the estate on the death of his father James. The Old Parochial Register for Stewarton records the death of a John Bell in December 1805, aged 91 years.

The road to Stewarton, running east, with the main entrance to Kennox House on the left and Kennox Lodge on the right. The photograph dates from 1908 when the lodge was occupied by the estate's coachman, William Cameron, a Dundonian, his Irish-born wife Elizabeth and their daughters, Dorothy and Alice. The North Gate Lodge (since demolished), stood at the estate's west entrance and was then home to a ploughman, David McKechnie.

Kersland House, Stewarton

On the east side of Stewarton's Vennel Street, Kersland House was built in 1855 for James Anderson Snodgrass (1803-1882) – confirmed by the inscription "S" "1855" on a shield built into the porch – his wife Margaret (1804-1883) and two of their seven children – Agnes (b.1832) and Thomas (b.1844). They had lived in Stewarton's Main Street. The son of Thomas Snodgrass, farmer, Lugton Rigs, Beith, James was a notary public, prosecutor at Ayr Sheriff Court, bank agent (Western Bank of Scotland and the Union Bank of Scotland) and agent for the Insurance Company of Scotland. Around 1830 he married Margaret Kerr, daughter of William Kerr a flesher in Stewarton, and as the house was initially named Kerrsland, may suggest its derivation. Neither the architect nor the builder is known but Snodgrass was born in Beith suggesting that Robert Snodgrass, architect and builder there, who built a similar villa on Beith's Dalry Road – and the Wallace monument at Barnweil (1855-1857) – was responsible. The housing development Kersland Gait was built in its grounds in 1996.

Kilmarnock House, Kilmarnock

Kilmarnock's 'Ragged School', on the north side of St. Marnock Street, in 1902. The original 17th century building fronted north onto what is now Nelson Street, with a later extension to the left, or west side and its land extending south into today's Howard Park.

In 1735, whilst William, 4th Earl of Kilmarnock (born 1704), was in Europe, fire broke out at Dean Castle forcing his wife, Lady Anne, daughter of James, 5th Earl of Linlithgow, and their children to move to Kilmarnock House. Alas, William picked the wrong side in the Jacobite Rebellion and, captured at the Battle of Culloden, was executed at Tower Hill, London in August 1746. In 1855 the house became the Kilmarnock Ragged and Industrial Certified School – one of eighteen such schools in Scotland caring for 2,669 children – managed by thirteen patrons, 34 directors, a general purposes committee of six, an admissions committee of five and a committee 'for the settlement of pupils leaving' of four – with twelve boys and twelve girls. By 1873 numbers had increased to 44 boys and 28 girls, one of whom was Elizabeth M'Ewan. The daughter of John M'Ewan, a bonegatherer, Elizabeth was committed to the school for eight years by Kilmarnock Police Court in April 1870, due to inadequate guardianship; her mother having died, her father had left her, unprovided for, in the keeping of strangers. In 1879, 28 children were hospitalised with typhoid. At the time of this photograph, the superintendent was 53 year old William McMenan (son of John McMenan, a Christian Missionary) with his wife Margaret as matron, caring for 79 boys and 29 girls, ranging in age from seven years to fifteen years. Less than half were Ayrshire-born, the others coming from Glasgow and Lanarkshire, Renfrewshire, Edinburgh, Forfarshire and Ross-shire. It closed in 1920 and Lord Howard de Walden gifted the building, and the quandary of what to do with it, to Kilmarnock Town Council. After years of discussion, and a proposal to convert it to a town hall, it was demolished in 1935 – much of the stone going to the new gatehouse at Dean Castle – creating the car park we know today. A model of the house is on display at Dean Castle, Kilmarnock.

A broadside portrait of William Boyd, 4th Earl of Kilmarnock, printed and sold at his execution, by beheading, at Tower Hill, London on 18th August 1746, aged 42 years. The execution of Arthur Elphinstone, 6th Lord Balmerino, also captured at the Battle of Culloden, followed. The final two beheadings carried out in the United Kingdom were, Charles Radclyffe (8th December 1746) and Simon Fraser, Lord Lovat (9th April 1747), also Jacobites. Boyd's widow, Lady Anne Livingstone, daughter of James, 5th Earl of Linlithgow, survived him by one year and one month, dying at Kilmarnock House on 18th September 1747 of, it is said, a broken heart.

Kingencleuch House, Mauchline

The north facing front of Kingencleuch House in the early 1930s, the central section being that built by John Campbell of Kingencleuch (d.1752), on leaving the castle, which stands to the south, to fall into ruin. The extension to the left dates from 1777, with that to the right coming later. The Consolidated Schedules of Assessed Taxes for 1798-99 (vol. 4) (Ayrshire) shows the estate proprietor as Mrs. McGill, who paid £19.14s. (fifteen windows, one male servant, one four wheel carriage, two horses and one dog) tax that year. Mrs. Margaret McGill *née* Campbell, daughter of John was the last of the Campbell family, who married David McGill, but was widowed at his death in August 1767. She died in May 1808 and the Inventory and Deed of Settlement of her estate, lodged at Glasgow in 1812, includes the sum of £3,000 in a personal bond (undated) by Claud Alexander of Ballochmyle (who had died in 1809), for the purchase of Kingencleuch. The Ordnance Survey of 1855 records that it was, *A plain comfortable villa occasionally occupied by Mr. Alexander when visiting his Ballochmyle estate*. It is still owned by the family (2017).

In 1957 Sir Claud Hagart-Alexander (1927-2006), the 3rd Bart, had the house restored and remodelled by the Glasgow architect Mervyn Noad, adding the two storey porch. During the Second World War the field to the west of the house was commandeered and became Prisoner of War Camp no. 112 under the administration of the camp at Doonfoot, Ayr. The satellite image of the field shows the marks of its many huts, one of which survives in the yard of Kingencleuch Farm. From 1949 into the 1950s the camp was home to some of the 20,000 Ukrainians brought to this country under the European Voluntary Workers Scheme.

Kirkland Park House, Darvel

In 1880 the 37 year old lace manufacturer Alexander Morton and his wife Janet Bryce, who married in 1863, had Kirkland Park built on the east side of the track leading to Law Quarry, north of Darvel – its gated driveway off East Main Street is now Robertson Gardens. Their entwined initials were carved into the porch lintel. At the birth of their son, Robert Alexander Morton, in 1868, they lived at 2 Hastings Place, Darvel. Simultaneous with the building of Kirkland Park, another Alexander Morton (1844-1923), also a lace manufacturer, and perhaps a cousin, was building Gowanbank to the west of Darvel. Janet died in 1910, and on Alexander's death in 1921, aged 78 years, tenancy passed to his daughter-in-law, Agnes Bowie, widow of Dr. Robert A Morton, who died in January 1928. By the 1940s it was occupied, for a time, by John Connell of the printing and publishing business Walker and Connell in Darvel's Hastings Square. In 1984 Strathclyde Regional Council relinquished it as an assessment centre for young offenders and set it on the road to ruin and decay – a fire in February 2010 sealing its fate.

The front of the house in 2015 – as nature encroaches.

Lainshaw House, Stewarton

Lainshaw House in the early 1900s. Surviving drawings by the architect George Washington Browne (1853-1939), who made small additions to the property in 1898, detail that the apartments on the ground floor, from left to right, were: a cloakroom, the entry hallway, the butler's pantry and, in the Gothic extension, the kitchen, scullery and larder. At the heart of the building is a tower house, which could date to 1283 when the 4,300 acre estate, extending over the parishes of Stewarton, Dunlop and Riccarton, was known as the Lordship of Stewarton, and held by the Stewart family. In 1450 King James II granted the land to Alexander Home of Holme, it eventually passing to Neil Montgomerie, the 2nd son of Hugh Montgomerie (1460-1545) the 1st Earl of Eglinton, who became the 1st Laird of Langshaw (Lainshaw). The succession ran to the 10th Laird, Sir Walter Montgomerie-Cuninghame (d.1814) a 'Tobacco Baron' who lost his fortune in the American Revolutionary War (1775-1783).

The east entry to the estate, photographed around 1906, was probably built for William Cunninghame in the early 1780s. In the 1920s a second storey was added to each lodge and in the 1950s, when the council housing on David Dale Avenue was built (Ayrshire County Council owning the house and grounds may have eased any planning difficulties), the gates and piers were removed and, at a later date, the lodges extended.

Lainshaw House, Stewarton

The house viewed from the south bank of the Annick Water in the 1930s, when owned by the Glasgow stockbroker and accountant William Henry Goff, who had bought it in April 1920 from Richard J Cunninghame. Goff died in 1943, and in 1947 Ayrshire County Council purchased the house and grounds, converting it to a home accommodating 45 old people. To the purchase price of £8,000, renovations added £14,000 and furniture £7,000. In 1993 up-grading costs forced its closure and abandonment to decay and vandalism until a planning application, from Travis Homes, to restore and convert it to eleven flats, with 37 houses in the grounds, was lodged with East Ayrshire Council in June 2005, and approved.

Lanfine House, Newmilns

Lanfine estate, and Waterhaughs to its north-west, was in the hands of the Church until the Reformation when, recorded as the lands of Lenfene, it came to the Campbells of Cessnock. In 1769 it was acquired by John Brown (1729-1802) of the Glasgow banking firm Carrick, Brown & Co. (later the Ship Bank, 9 Glassford Street, Glasgow) who had the north facing, central part of the house, with its bow windows, built, employing, tradition says, the Mauchline mason James Armour, father-in-law of the poet Robert Burns. Armour is also credited with the construction of the Howford Bridge, Skeldon House and Dalmellington Parish Church. The estate passed to Brown's son Nicol (b.1768), who was also with the bank, and on his death in 1829 at Waterhaughs, to his cousin Dr. Thomas Brown (1774-1853) of Langside, Glasgow. With the new owner came extensions to the house, the bridge over the Newlands Burn, the lodges and the walled garden with its conservatory. The estate passed to his son Thomas, an advocate, and on his death in 1873, to his daughter Martha, whose death in 1897, aged 89 years, ended 128 years of the family's ownership of the estate.

In 1902 Thomas Neil McKinnon, a retired iron merchant from James Watson & Co., bought the estate, but his bankruptcy in 1910 returned it to the market, when it was bought, the following year, by the shipping magnate, Sir Charles Cayzer (1843-1916) for his son, Herbert Robin Cayzer (1881-1958), 1st Baron Rotherwick. It remained with the family until 1967.

The south-facing conservatory within the two acre walled garden, to the east of the house, was built for Dr. Thomas Brown (1774-1853) in the early 1830s. Having studied medicine at Edinburgh University, he was a lecturer of botany at Glasgow University from 1799 until 1815. It produced abundant crops of peaches, nectarines and figs, but was abandoned in the late 1960s. The illustration shows only the conservatory and the formal garden fronting it, with the kitchen gardens, out of view, on either side.

Bridge and Temple   Lanfine

Lanfine Fountain

Built around 1830, this single arch bridge carries the driveway over the Newlands Burn towards the East Lodge and Ranoldcoup Road with, on the skyline, the 'Temple', a summer house, long since demolished.

The cast iron fountain in the garden at Lanfine was manufactured in the 1870s at Andrew Handyside's Britannia Foundry in Derby. Its hexagonal base, with a lion's head on each face, leads to an acanthus leaf stem supporting the main bowl, out of which three entwined dolphins balance the upper bowl which, in turn, is topped by two cherubs – taking it to a height of 14' 4 ½". It may seem a long way to transport such a heavy garden feature, but at this time the roof of St. Enoch Railway Station in Glasgow was also coming north from Handyside's foundry, and it had a span of 205 feet and a length of 525 feet.

Loch Doon Castle (Balloch Castle) (Baliol Castle), Dalmellington

The 13th century castle on Castle Island, Loch Doon, in 1911. It is not known who built the castle, perhaps the ancient Lords of Carrick, but there is a record of it affording refuge to Sir Christopher Seton, a brother-in-law of Robert Bruce, after the Battle of Methven (19th June 1306), when in the hands of Sir Gilbert de Carrick. The English forces took the castle and hanged Seton, as a traitor, at Dumfries. The base of the irregular, eleven sided, curtain wall measured 91 feet from east to west and 80 feet north to south, stood 26 feet high and ranged in thickness between seven and nine feet. Searches for the castle's portcullis, in 1823 and 1831, were partially successful when six dug-out canoes, two of which were given to Glasgow's Hunterian Museum, were found. Another, found in 1911, disintegrated when taken from the water.

Interior of Balloch Castle, Loch Doon, Dalmellington.

The four storey rubble-built keep inside the west wall had a base measuring 35 feet by 22 feet, and was of a later date. It was not removed in 1935 and remains under the water of the loch.

The first modern threat to the castle came in 1916 when the outflow of the River Doon, at the north end of the loch, was dammed for a hydro-electric scheme to power the £400,000, later abandoned, Loch Doon School of Aerial Gunnery, raising the water level by six feet. However, the Galloway Water Power Act of 1929 initiated a £3 million scheme to use Loch Doon as a seasonal reservoir for the generating stations at Kendoon, Carsfad, Earlston and Tongland, through a system of tunnels. The new dam would raise the loch surface by 30 feet – and endanger the castle. In August 1935, under the supervision of the Edinburgh architect James Smith Richardson (1883-1970) acting for H.M. Office of Works, the wall was photographed, before each stone was numbered and again photographed, and removed to the west bank, where it was reconstructed. This photograph, from the east side of the loch, shows the work in progress.

The castle is shown on a detail of the *New Map of Ayrshire, comprehending Kyle, Cunningham & Carrick. The Scale, one Inch to a Mile* surveyed 1773-1774 by the cartographer Captain Andrew Armstrong (1712-1784) of the Royal Army Engineers, and his son Mostyn John Armstrong (1765-1791). It was engraved onto copper by Stephen Pyle, Angel Court, Snow Hill, London, in 1774.

Lochridge House, Stewarton

The earliest record of Lochridge, or Lochrig as it then was, dates to 1417 when, according to *Paterson's History of the County of Ayrshire*, John de Arnot of Lochrig was listed as a juror in a dispute between the Burgh of Irvine and William Fraunces of Stane. The estate appears on *Blaeu's Atlas of Scotland* (1654) and a house is evident on Armstrong's map of 1775. The house, and its seven acres of land, remained in the Arnot family until 1741 when Jean Galt Arnot married Matthew Stewart of Newton, and was with the Stewart family until 1830 when it came to David Provan, a 49 year old, Killearn-born, retiree from the Honourable East India Company Service, having served as surgeon to the rulers of the state of Travancore in south India. That same year he married Emma, the 18 year old daughter of William Reid, a bookseller in Glasgow. His death in December 1851 brought the succession to his son, also David (1834-1903), who built this new house around the core of the old. In May 1920 the house and its estate, including Wardhead House (now, 2017, the premises of Kingspan Wind, the wind turbine manufacturer), with the farms Horsemuir, Lochside and Byrahill, was bought by the Glasgow diamond merchant Thomas Henderson Gollan of Hector Gollan & Son. At his death in August 1934, the estate was managed by trustees before being sold as individual properties.

Logan House, Cumnock

Logan estate's recorded history goes back to William Logan, a Writer to the Signet, of Restalrig, Edinburgh, who purchased the 1,000 acre estate in the 1660s. Armstrong's 1775 *New Map of Ayrshire*, shows a house on the estate but the building of the one illustrated here, was only started around 1798 by Hugh Logan (1739-1803) and unfinished at his death. An unmarried father, several times over, Logan lost with the collapse of Douglas, Heron & Co.'s bank in 1772 and is remembered as a wit – his many 'wisdoms' later published as *The Laird of Logan – being anecdotes and Tales illustrative of the Wit and Humour of Scotland*. Over the centuries, his brand of humour has paled. In 1949 the house was demolished, and the estate passed to the Scottish Special Housing Association, becoming the 'village' of Logan with the building of 142 houses.

Loudoun Castle, Galston

Deemed one of Ayrshire's finest mansions, Loudoun Castle was built around a 17th century core, to plans by the architect Archibald Elliot (1760-1823) and his brother James (1770-1810), specialists in castellated, Gothic style, country houses. Commissioned by the 6th Countess, Flora Mure-Campbell (1780-1840) the work spanned the years 1804 to 1811, whilst the Elliots were also engaged with Stobo Castle in Peeblesshire, Perthshire's Taymouth Castle and Dreghorn Castle, Edinburgh. This 1880s photograph shows the west facing front, carriage ramp and entrance which opened into a hall measuring 70 feet by 30 feet wide, open to the roof, and giving access to the castle's 90 apartments. In the early hours of 1st December 1941 the 12th Countess, Edith Maud Rawdon-Hastings (1883-1960), was awakened by the noise of crackling timber and the smell of burning – there was fire in the first floor library, above her bedroom. Rousing her daughters, Countess Lady Jean Wakefield and her infant daughter and Lady Edith Hastings, who were in adjoining rooms, they escaped minutes before the library ceiling collapsed. The building, and its contents, was lost and remains the shell created that morning. The family was descended from James de Loudon, who had obtained the lands and barony from Richard de Morvelle, High Constable of Scotland to King David II. The Loudoun earldom dates from 1601, the first Earl of Loudoun being Sir John Campbell, Chancellor for Scotland. Between 1995 and 2010 a theme park operated in the castle grounds.

The gatekeeper's cottage, photographed in the 1890s, stood on the north side of the drive from the castle, to the Galston–Moscow road, with Byresbank Plantation on the right and Orchard Plantation to the left. To the right, out of scene, was the track to Byres, described in the *Ordnance Survey Name Book* (1855-1857) as *Old buildings occupied by Cottagers the property of the Marquis of Hastings*. The cottage is not itemised in the valuation roll, but features in the 1881 census, when occupied by 38 year old George Nisbet, a general labourer (d.1883) and his wife Ann. The census also shows that the castle had 84 'rooms with one or more windows' – the gatehouse had one. It was demolished around 1953.

The original entry to the castle was on the east side, before Elliot's creation moved it to the west front.

Mansfield House, New Cumnock

The Edinburgh Advertiser of 25th June 1816 carried a notice for the sale of an 'Extensive and Improvable Estate in Ayrshire' – Mansfield and Castlemains. Mansfield had a small mansion house close to the Lynn Burn and was bounded, for three and a half miles to the south, by the River Nith, with Castlemains on the south bank. The previous owner, Andrew Thomson, a Glasgow merchant with interests in Greenock, had died in July 1806 leaving his wife, Margaret, with life-rental of the house and estate. The income from land rent was £1,730 per annum, and coal and lime returned £200. In 1824 it was bought by Sir Charles Granville Stuart-Menteath (1769-1847) of Closeburn, Dumfriesshire, whose work as an agricultural improver was rewarded with a baronetage in 1838. Initially he installed his factor, John Wallace, on the estate. The house was enlarged by either Sir Charles or his son, Sir James Stuart-Menteath (1792-1870), but was never more than a shooting lodge encircled by coalworks and limeworks. Sir Charles died at the family's winter house at 27 Abercrombie Place, Edinburgh in December 1847. In September 1937, Sir William Frederick Stuart-Menteath, 5th Baronet (1874-1952) had the property marketed by the Edinburgh estate agents Walker, Fraser & Steele. Their advertisement shows its accommodation as; four reception rooms, six bedrooms, three maids rooms, a modern kitchen with Aga cooker, a five car garage, walled garden, tennis court, seven cottages and six farms, covering 2,320 acres. The house was demolished in the late 1950s.

Mauchline Castle (Abbot Hunter's Tower), Mauchline

The name Mauchline Castle is a misnomer, it being merely a tower. The 'Castle' dates from the mid 15th century and its alternative name Abbot Hunter's Tower, may refer to Abbot Andrew Hunter (1444-71). This early 20th century photograph, from the bleaching green to its north-east, includes Gavin Hamilton's house, on the left. Hamilton (1751-1805), a writer (lawyer), was a friend of and an early supporter of the poet Robert Burns. Today, this view is partially obscured by the 1894 built hall of Mauchline Parish Church, and with the battlements and chimney on the left already gone, the whole structure is creeping into decay.

Milrig House, Galston

Built by Bruce Campbell of Milrig, Mayfield and Hillhouse, Milrig House stood on the east side of the Galston to Crosshands road, and features on Armstrong's 1775 map of Ayrshire and the Carriage Tax Roll for 1786, which shows Campbell's two wheeled carriage cost him £3.10s. per annum. The agricultural improvers, Matthew and George Culley write of Campbell in their *Travel Journals and Letters*, (1765-1798) – *we proceeded next to Bruce Campbell Esq. of Millrigg, a man of considerable understanding, but rather backward in his improvements*. When 79 year old Campbell died in February 1813, the 346 acre Milrig estate included the dairy farms of Sornhill and Millside, and was occupied by Lieutenant General John Hughes of Balkissock, who died at Mountcharles, Co. Donegal in April 1832. It was bought by Captain Alexander Duncan Tait of the 4th Regiment Dragoon Guards, who had it re-modelled to the commodious residence containing four reception rooms and ten bedrooms with dressing rooms, in the photograph. Alexander died at the Sackville Hotel, Sackville Street, London in January 1881, leaving his widow, Marion, who survived until 1888. Noted for her benevolence, she provided bread and soup over the winter months for 70 of Galston's poorest. Their son, Colonel John Sprot Tait, having served with the 12th Lancers, succeeded to the estate, and was a Justice of the Peace and Depute Lieutenant of Ayrshire until his death in 1924. The estate was sold the following year, and again in 1933, when it was divided, 60 acres remaining with the house and the remainder going to the two farms. It was demolished in the late 20th century and a new house built on its site.

Netherplace House, Mauchline

The west facing front of Netherplace, around 1900, from the driveway leading to the arched gateway on Loudoun Street opposite Barskimming Road. The early history of the estate is uncertain, but Robertson writes that he has *seen a document, dated 1569, by Mungo, eldest lawful son of Mungo Campbell of Brownside, to his brother, Hugh, of the lands of Ten-shilling-side, and others, now called Netherplace.* This house was built by William Campbell (1772-1843), who laid the foundation stone on 14th April 1827, replacing a tower house which stood a short distance to the north. He was the last 'Campbell' laird of Netherplace, dying on Christmas Day 1843 when he was succeeded by his sister Margaret (1771-1847), and on her death, by his second sister Lillias, who passed away on 20th April 1851. There being no direct heir, the estate was left to a board of trustees comprising of: Lieut-Colonel John Ferrier Hamilton of Cairnhill, Walter Riddell, merchant in London; Charles Dalrymple Gardner, banker in Kilmarnock; Charles Vereker Hamilton of the Honourable East India Company Service and Robert Gardner, banker in Kilmarnock. The following year, Charles Vereker Hamilton, now Campbell, petitioned the Court of Session for authority for a conveyance of Netherplace to John Ferrier Hamilton of Cairnhill (his father), who died in 1871, for the sum of £20,000, which was granted. The estate was with the Hamilton-Campbells until the death of Mungo in 1953, when it was sold to the Alexanders of Ballochmyle. The house was demolished in January 1957, and outline planning for a residential development on its site was granted by Ayr County Council. In March 2000 East Ayrshire Council granted permission for the erection of 56 houses.

Newmilns Tower, Newmilns

The Irvine Valley is unusual in having two neighbouring towns with surviving tower houses – Barr Castle in Galston and Newmilns Tower – one a masonic lodge and the other a private dwelling. The three storey, rubble built, Newmilns Tower in Castle Street, to the rear of the Loudoun Arms public house, is believed to have been built in the 1530s by Sir Hew Campbell of Loudoun, and sacked in a raid by the Kennedys of Dunure. Its base is 30 feet by 24 feet and the five feet thick walls are topped by a parapet 30 feet above. It has served as a prison for Covenanters and a stable, with hay and corn lofts, for the adjacent inn. To the right of the entrance are the slit windows of the wheel stair and on the top floor, two shot holes. Between 1994 and 1996, with funding from the Architectural Heritage Fund, Scottish Development Agency, Historic Scotland and Enterprise Ayrshire, the building and its grounds underwent an archaeological investigation and renovation, before being sold as a private dwelling.

Ochiltree House, Ochiltree

The late 17th century built Ochiltree House, part of Auchinleck estate, photographed in the early 20th century when occupied by the coalmaster James Angus and his family. The 1901 census lists the residents as James Angus (37), coalmaster, his 34 year old, New Zealand-born wife Elizabeth, and their three children; Robert (6), Caroline (4) and Jean (2), with seven servants. James died in the house in December 1902. In the First World War Robert, a captain with No. 64 Squadron of the Royal Flying Corps, was killed in aerial combat over the battlefield of Cambrai on 20th November 1917. The original house, or castle, in which the Reformer John Knox (c.1514-1572) married Margaret Stewart, the 17 year old daughter of Andrew, 2nd Lord Stewart of Ochiltree, in 1564, was lost to a fire in 1680 and this house was built to replace it – the ruins of the old house survived, in the garden, into the 20th century. The Ordnance Survey of the 1850s describes it as – *A plain lofty building 3 storeys high Slated with Crowstep gables on all other respects a plain Common building in very bad repair.* Despite its poor condition, it stood another century until its demolition in March 1952, bequeathing its name to the house built on the site in 1972.

Polquhairn House, Ochiltree

In the late 1890s Polquhairn House was occupied by the bachelor farmer James Pettigrew Wilson (d.1899), his housekeeper, Jane McDonald, and his farm and house servants. It appears on Armstrong's map of 1775 as Dalquharn, when occupied by Adam Craufurd Newall, son of David Newall of Knockreoch in Kirkcudbrightshire who, two years earlier had lost £500 with the collapse of the Ayr Bank, Douglas, Heron & Co. Newall died in June 1790 and the 1,600 acre estate, including the farms Piperhill, Elymains, Muirston and Steelpark, was sold to Hugh Ross of Kerse who changed the name to Polquhairn. In 1805 it was sold to James Cuthbert, a wine merchant of Ayr's Academy Street, but a report in the *Edinburgh Mercury* of 7th April 1806 suggests that Cuthbert was also working from home; *We hear, that a few days since, Mr. Gillies, Supervisor of Excise, Ayr, and Mr. Erskine, officer, discovered an illegal distillery in the house of Polquhairn, parish of Ochiltree. They seized and carried off the still and utensils, together with a quantity of aquavitae, which they found secreted in the drawing room and in the chaise.*

Robertland House, Stewarton

On the south side of the Old Glasgow Road (now the B769) out of Stewarton, Robertland was a 2,243 acre estate, and six storey house, owned by Sir William Cunningham of Livingston until the 1780s when it was acquired by Sir James Hunter-Blair (1741-1787) of Dunskey. Around 1813 it was bought by Alexander Kerr (1775-1847), a native of Stewarton, having made his fortune in American tobacco. In 1820, to plans attributed to the Glasgow architect David Hamilton, who later worked on nearby Dunlop House, Robertland House was built on the north bank of the Swinzie Burn. Alexander was succeeded by his son, John James (1822-1900), but as he lived at Ardgare House, Helensburgh, Robertland was let to a succession of tenants. Early on the morning of Thursday, 12th March 1914, a farm worker saw fire through the trees and raised the alarm. As the fire engine at Kilmarnock was an hour away, estate workers passed buckets of water, hand to hand, from a pump at the rear of the house, but it was too little, too late. The following year's valuation roll records the house as 'burned down' – its rebuilding was many years ahead. Overnight snow recorded two sets of female footprints coming from the conservatory, where a pane of glass had been removed to access the house, and on the driveway were two brown paper wrapped postcards – one inscribed *Release Mrs. Pankhurst* and the other *Now is the time for the Church to show its independence of the state. R.I.P.*. Mrs. Emmeline Pankhurst, leader of the Women's Social & Political Union (the Suffragettes), had been arrested at a Suffragettes meeting, in Glasgow's St. Andrew's Hall on the Monday evening, but there were no arrests for the wilful fireraising at Robertland.

The estate's lodge on the Old Glasgow Road around 1913 when occupied by the gamekeeper, William Bruce. It first appears on the 1894 Ordnance Survey map having been built when the driveway was re-aligned.

The 62 yard square walled garden, with its lean-to greenhouse, stands to the east of the house and is probably contemporary with it. Much, if not all, of the stone for its wall came from the castle, including a marriage stone IR * AR, celebrating the marriage of James VI of Scotland and Anne of Denmark in 1587, over the entry. The connection is unclear, but following the murder of Hugh, 4th Earl of Eglinton in April 1586, David Cunningham of Robertland, who may have been involved in the killing, was banished to Denmark.

The footbridge in Robertland Glen, over the Swinzie Burn, as it flows west between Robertland Castle to the south and Robertland House to the north, to join the Annick Water.

Rodinghead House, Mauchline

In the late 18th century, George Douglas (d.1826), factor to the Duke of Portland, and then living at Loudoun Castle, added the 131 acre Rodinghead estate, formerly part of the Lordship of Kylesmuir, to his portfolio of properties, and in 1805 built the nucleus of today's house. The architect is not known. Business interests brought him into partnership with James Fairlie of Bellfield, Mungo Fairlie of Holmes, Patrick Ballantine of Castlehill, Ayr, and William Parker of Assloss, in founding the Kilmarnock Banking Company (1802-1820). His image survives in a painting (auctioned at Southeby's, to a private collector in 1993 for £3,800) by the portraitist Henry Raeburn (1756-1823) which, with the estate, passed to his only son (he had four daughters; Isabella, Elizabeth, Flora and Jean), also George (1800-1850), a solicitor with Douglas & Hamilton, King Street, Kilmarnock. On his death the estate passed to his wife, Anne Campbell, daughter of Hugh Campbell of Mayfield, whom he had married at Radford, Nottinghamshire in February 1829, and on her passing, at Havelock Terrace (now part of Miller Road), Ayr, in January 1885, aged 85 years, to Douglas's sister, Elizabeth, wife of Captain Francis Hay of the 34th Regiment of Infantry.

Rowallan Castle, Kilmaurs

Rowallan Castle, with the building contractors John Boyd and Robert Forrest, who carried out the renovation work on it whilst building the new 'castle' and lodge house, between 1903 and 1905. The late 16th century castle, with its distinctive twin drum towers and 22 step stairway, has the remnants of much earlier buildings to its rear. It is recorded in the 1855-57 *Ordnance Survey Name Book*, when it was … *going fast to decay and only a few apartments are occupied by the Woodman, Robert Dale* – the 1900 advertisement for the estate says … *The Castle would lend itself readily to restoration.* Born in the castle in 1825, Robert Dale served five successive Earls of Loudoun as forester, and died there in December 1910, aged 84 years. He planted the large tree to the right of the stairway.

Built concurrently with the new house, and in the same style, Rowallan's two storey lodge house stands on the north side of the Kilmaurs to Fenwick road. Though most estates had lodges, few were on the scale of Rowallan's.

The front of the new house.

When advertised for sale on behalf of the Earl of Loudoun in May 1900, Rowallan Estate generated little interest. It went to auction at Tokenhouse Yard, London in September 1901, and was bought by Archibald Cameron Corbett, the Member of Parliament for Glasgow, Tradeston (1886-1911), for £140,000 (upset price £150,000). The estate had 4,490 acres of arable land, divided amongst 37 farms (mostly dairy), 1,485 acres of moorland (well stocked with game) and 105 acres of mature woodland. The gross rental amounted to £6,349, and the public and parochial burdens came to £454. Corbett was the son of a Glasgow merchant and in 1887, aged 21 years, married Alice Mary Polson, the daughter of John Polson, co-founder of Brown & Polson, the corn flour manufacturer of Paisley. Alice died at their London home in Hans Place, in July 1902, aged 45 years, and was interred on Harelaw Muir, west of Kingswell, where a memorial cross was later erected, and where Arthur would join her in 1933. The Edinburgh architect, Sir Robert Stodart Lorimer (1864-1929), was commissioned to design the new house, the lodge, stables, coach houses and motor car sheds, and the contractors, Boyd & Forrest of Kilmarnock, completed the transformation from drawings to reality in 1905 at a cost of £28,172. The dressed stone was brought from Northumberland but the rubble was, as with that of the castle, quarried locally. The *London Gazette* of 11th July 1911, announced: *Archibald Cameron Corbett, Esquire and the male heirs of his body lawfully begotten, by the name, style and title of Baron Rowallan of Rowallan, in the county of Ayr* – marking both his retiral from Parliament and the accession of King George V. They had three children. Thomas Godfrey Polson Corbett (1895-1977), the 2nd Baron, served part of the First World War with the Ayrshire Yeomanry at Gallipoli, was Chief Scout (1945-1959), and Governor of Tasmania (1959-1963). Elsie Cameron Corbett (1896-1976), was with the British Red Cross in Serbia (1915-1919), a Justice of the Peace in Oxfordshire, and on her death was buried at All Saints Church, Spelsbury, Oxfordshire. Arthur Cameron Corbett (b.1898) was killed on 4th December 1916, flying a Sopwith Pup out of Dunkirk, with No. 8 Squadron, Royal Naval Air Service, and buried at Heilly Station Cemetery, Mericourt L'Abbé, France.

John Boyd (1825-1911) & Robert Forrest (1846-1917)

Born in 1825, John Boyd served his apprenticeship with his father, a builder in Kilmaurs, before starting on his own account. His first major work was an office building for the coalmasters, Messrs. Finnie & Sons on the north-west corner of Kilmarnock's John Finnie Street and Grange Place, with Robert Forrest as his site overseer. A native of Kirriemuir, Angus, Forrest was a journeyman mason who had come to Kilmarnock seeking work. Not only did he find work with Boyd, but also a wife when, aged 25, he married his employer's 23 year old daughter Janet, in December 1871. They formed a partnership, operating initially from Stewarton, then the disused Vulcan Foundry in Kilmarnock's West Langlands Street. Major projects included: Ayr Railway Station and Hotel, The King's Theatre, Kilmarnock, Glenbuck House and Rowallan. They were also railway contractors, at one time employing 1,500 men, building the G&SWR branch line from Newmilns to Darvel, and a loop line from Barleith, through Riccarton to Gatehead.

Skeldon House, Dalrymple

Built around 1760 for Hugh Ross (1695-1775) of Kerse and Skeldon, who had succeeded to the property on the death of his brother William in 1739, the latter having bought it six years earlier from Christina Crawford of Kerse for 18,000 Scots merks (the Scots merk was worth 2/3rds of a Scots pound or one English shilling). The stone was taken from the nearby, but then ruined, Kerse Castle. It was Nether Skeldon, and Hollybush was Over Skeldon. A remaining wall of the old castle was brought down on the night of 29th December 1797 by the storm which dispersed the French fleet anchored in Bantry Bay preparing for the invasion of Ireland. In 1801 the house was bought by John Fullarton of the Honourable East India Company Service at Patna, Bihar, India, where he died in June 1804, leaving his estate, including Skeldon, to his son, William (1774-1835), an advocate, and Provost of Ayr (1831-1835) when he died. Jane Cuming, wife of General the Honourable John Leslie, formerly of the Grenadier Guards, held the property until 1867, when it was bought by the Duke of Portland. For many years it was tenanted by Adam Wood, manager of the Duke's harbour at Troon. In 1908, whether at the expense of the Duke of Portland or Adam Wood, the Glasgow architect James Miller was commissioned to add a neo-Georgian single storey, domed roofed, semi-circular, entrance hall with four Ionic columns to the front and a conservatory to the rear. Concurrent with, and in contrast to, this commission, Miller was working on the North British Locomotive Company's offices at Springburn, Glasgow. In deference to the duke, the 11th hole on Royal Troon's Portland Course is named Skeldon. After Adam Wood died in 1917, the house was tenanted by his sister, Margaret. Skeldon was one of the 90 Ayrshire properties the Duke sold in 1919 and was bought by Margaret Wood who died in October 1923.

Sorn Castle, Sorn

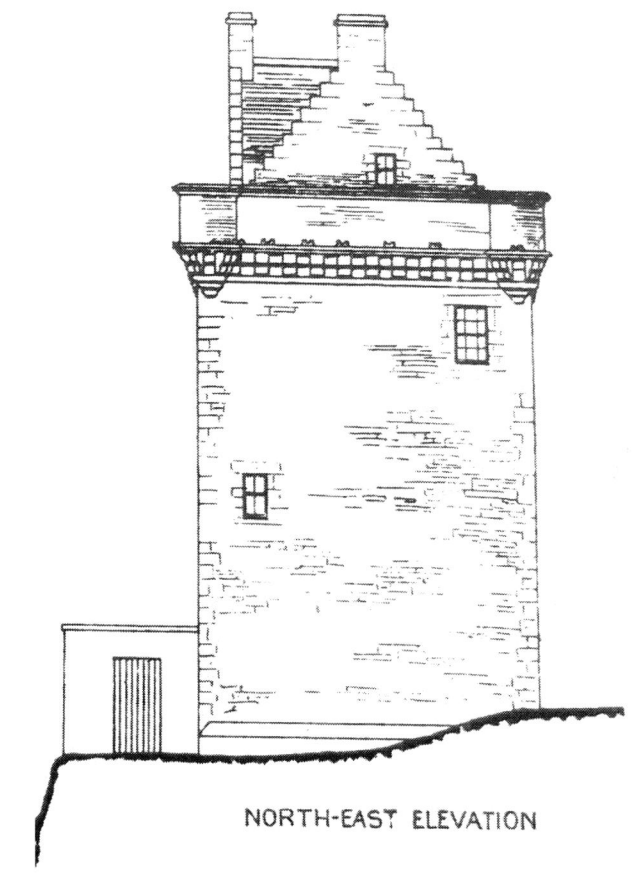

NORTH-EAST ELEVATION

SOUTH-EAST ELEVATION

MacGibbon and Ross in their 1887 book *The Castellated and Domestic Architecture of Scotland*, describe Sorn Castle as – *being of ancient fabric … situated on the crest of the precipitous bank of the River Ayr*. The estate dates from early times, perhaps with the Keiths of Galston in the 14th century. The Earl of Wintoun sold it to the Loudouns in the 17th century and they sold it to Dr. William Tennent of Pool (Poole, Pule) Farm, Carnwath, Lanarkshire, but recently returned from Bombay, in 1782. Renovation work he commissioned – adding a staircase and enlarging the drawing room – had just been completed when, in 1793, he married Janet, daughter of Sir James Dunbar of Mochrum (d.1782). Two years later, the Tennents sold the estate to William Somervell of Hamilton Farm, east of Rutherglen, and moved to London, where they died – he in 1807, and she in 1822.

This photograph of Sorn Castle was used by Alexander Hastie Millar in his book *The Castles and Mansions of Ayrshire* (pub.1885), when the estate was owned by James Somervell. The *Glasgow Directory* of 1799 lists – *Sommervill, William, of Sorn, lodging Miller Street*, a partner in the West Indies merchants, Somervell, Gordon & Co, who had bought the estate in 1795. He died "soon after", leaving his estate, including Hamilton Farm and the Sorn estate, to his wife, Jean *née* Cross and finally to his youngest daughter Agnes. She died, unmarried, at Sorn in 1856, aged 84 years. Graham Russell, then living at Clydehaughs, Govan, inherited the estate – and the surname Somervell. In tandem with making improvements to the house, his public services included Justice of the Peace, Deputy Lieutenant of the County and Convener of the County of Ayrshire. He also brought improvements to the house, doubling its size in 1864, with plans from the drawing board of the Edinburgh architect, David Bryce, and work by the Kilmarnock builder William Scott of Dundonald Road. At his death, in November 1881, the estate passed to his son James (1846-1924), a captain in the Ayrshire Yeomanry, and between 1890 and 1892 the MP for the Ayr Burghs – with the inherited civic duties of Justice of the Peace and Deputy Lieutenant of the County. Educated at Harrow and Oxford University, he was called to the Bar at the (English) Inner Temple in 1870. By 1900 he was bankrupt and the following year facing Sheriff-Substitute Campbell Shairp at Ayr, where he was stripped of the estate, and granted an allowance of £3.3s. per week. In August 1904 he appeared at the High Court of Justiciary, in Edinburgh, charged with an attempt to shoot one of the estate's trustees, Francis More, in his Edinburgh office, but was found not guilty. He died at Brixham, Torbay, Devon in February 1924.

With the estate in the hands of trustees, it was let annually for its sporting assets of fishing and shooting, and through 1908 and 1909 the silverware and paintings were auctioned. An attempt to sell it by auction at Messrs. Dowell's premises at 18 George Street, Edinburgh in August 1907 was unsuccessful, the advertisement describing it as … *the COMPACT RESIDENTIAL and SPORTING ESTATE of SORN, extends to 5452 acres, and includes about 1500 acres of moor and about 600 acres of woodland. The Shootings are excellent, 600 head of Game, excluding Rabbits, being killed last season. The house, which has recently been put in a good state of repair, Contains Five Public Rooms, Nine Bedrooms, Four Dressingrooms, Eight Servants' Rooms and Ample Kitchen Accommodation.* When Dowell offered it again, in November 1908, it was bought by Mr. Thomas Walker M'Intyre for £75,200. Before his death in September 1920, aged 60, McIntyre re-modelled the driveway, bringing it level with the front entry, over which he had a porte-cochere built, and added the viewing platform onto the River Ayr, seen in this illustration.

Templetonburn House, Kilmarnock.

Around 1900, 30 year old Robert Johnston Paton of the Kilmarnock seedsman and florist, W & T Samson, bought the 30 acre Templetonburn Farm, on the north side of what is now Milton Road, from William Cathcart Smith Cunninghame of Caprington, occupied by the farmer William Hamilton. Paton was then living at 44 Kay Park Crescent, Kilmarnock with his wife Helen, *née* Walker, whom he had married at her home, Crosbie Tower, Troon in 1893. He commissioned the architect, James Kennedy Hunter (1863-1929) of Ayr, to produce drawings for this Arts and Crafts / Scottish Baronial style house. By the autumn of 1901 the Patons, with their two elder sons, Robert (b.1894), Hugh (b.1898) were living in the house, with seven servants, the domestic gardener and his wife in the lodge, the coachman and his family in the stables, and three more gardeners in the bothy – the well-planted garden is a clue to Paton's profession. Two more sons, Alister and Thomas followed, in 1903 and 1906. The couple divorced in July 1923, and Paton died in the October, leaving the house to Helen, who was then Mrs. Helen

Goudie, Silverbeck, Churt, Farnham, Surrey. The property was rented, until bought, in the late 1930s, by the firebrick and fireclay manufacturer, William Frederick Charles Howie who died there in February 1957. In the 1960s, it was being converted to an hotel when it was destroyed by fire.

Thorntoun House, Kilmaurs

North of the Crosshouse to Dreghorn road, Thorntoun House and its 300 acre estate appear on Taylor and Skinner's illustrated survey of *The Road from Glasgow to Irvine*, published in February 1776, and captioned *Thornton – Capt Cunningham*. The early history of the estate, and the house, is uncertain. In June 1607 Margaret Ross, daughter of Robert Ross of Thorntoun, married Archibald Muir (possibly, later the Mures of Rowallan), a burgess of Glasgow. The Cuninghame family's association came in 1699, with the marriage of John Cuninghame (d.1753) of Caddell (near Ardrossan, Ayrshire) to Margaret, the eldest daughter of Sir Archibald Muir, and great-granddaughter of the Glasgow burgess. By the 1890s it was in the hands of George Edward Bourchier Wray (1851-1926) of Caddell and Thorntoun, who had married into the Cunningham family. He leased the house to the Glasgow iron merchant George Findlay Loudon (d. October 1914 at Orangefield, Monkton). The next tenant, who later bought the estate, was John Guthrie Sturrock, coalmaster and his wife Margaret *née* Finnie, daughter of the coalmaster Archibald Finnie of Springhill House, Kilmarnock. Born in 1854, he was the son of Peter Sturrock, Provost of Kilmarnock (1874-1886) – hence Sturrock Street – and Member of Parliament (1885-86) for Kilmarnock. John was a councillor with Ayrshire County Council, and Honorary Colonel of the 1st Ayrshire and Galloway Volunteer Artillery. Following his death in 1925, Margaret lived in the house until her passing, 22 years later, at the age of 91, bequeathing it for a nurses' home. The house was demolished and a residential school for Dr. Barnardo's Homes was built on the site in 1971. Today (2017) it serves the other end of life's spectrum as a care home for the elderly.

Tour House, Kilmaurs

The 115 acre Tour estate, including Kirkland Farm and Kirkton Cottages was granted to Robert Cuninghame of Robertland by the Abbott of Kelso in 1532, remaining in the family until 1840 when it was bought by the Glasgow merchant Robert Parker Adam (1799-1860), who built this house, on the site of its predecessor, to drawings by the Kilmarnock architect James Ingram. Adam married Margaret Haldane, daughter of James Haldane of Auchans, Dundonald, at Kilmarnock, in 1832. Their son, William Parker Adam (1839-1910), who succeeded him in the business, was born at Meadow Park House in Glasgow's Duke Street. In 1846 Adam was appointed a director of the Glasgow, Dumfries and Carlisle Railway Company and from 1857 was on the board of the Edinburgh and Glasgow Bank. James George Findlay (1855-1914), a retired merchant of the Irrawaddy Flotilla Company, Burma, bought the Tudor-Gothic style house and estate in 1903. His family occupied it until the 1930s when it became home to Major Ernest Guy Richard Lloyd (1890-1987), DSO, the Scottish Unionist Member of Parliament for East Renfrewshire from 1940 until 1959.

The driveway, running down to the north lodge, on the Kilmaurs to Kilmarnock road after it bridges the burn, around 1906. The lodge and the bridge are contemporary with the house, and survive. It was home to one of the estate's gardeners, George Rillie, born Dailly, Ayrshire around 1870 (died, Gourock, 1962), his Cullen-born wife Catherine and their three sons; John, b.1902 at Drumblade, Aberdeenshire, George, b.1905 at Prestonpans and Reginald born at Kilmaurs in 1910. A similar lodge at the south entrance was demolished in the late 1890s, although its foundations were extant until the early 1970s.

The walled garden with the conservatory, vinery, peach-house and melon-house to the right.

The gardener, George Rillie, tending the herbaceous border in the walled garden.

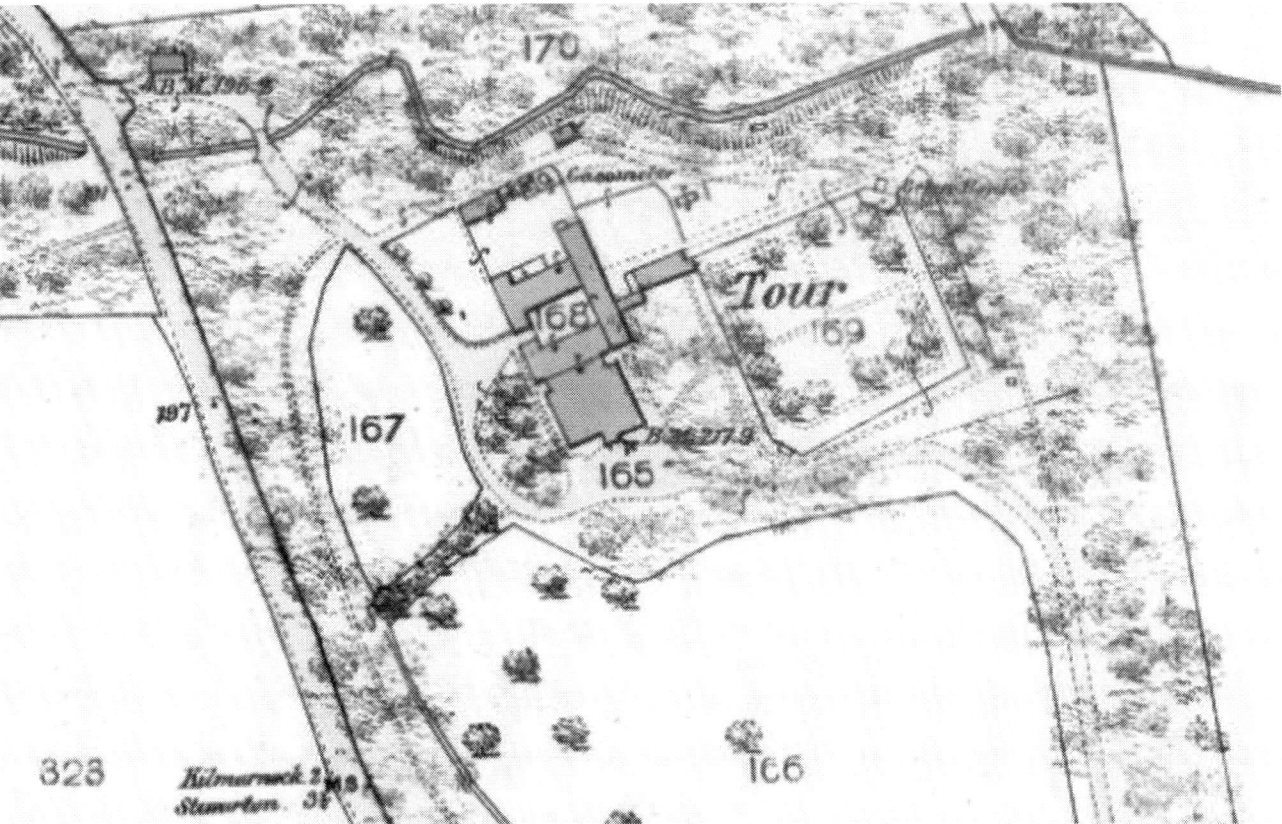

The Ordnance Survey map of 1856 shows a gasometer in the north-east corner of the outbuildings and, presumably, the apparatus to manufacture the coal gas. It would have been installed when Robert Parker Adam built the new house in 1840. Despite the initial cost, it would have been more economic than candles or oil lamps.

Treesbank House, Riccarton

The West Lodge to Treesbank estate on the Kilmarnock to Ayr road, around 1905 – the East Lodge was on the Kilmarnock to Craigie road, now Loreny Drive – when occupied by the estate's under gardner, Andrew Smillie. The house is long since demolished, although the bridge over Simon's Burn survives.

Once part of Cessnock estate, Treesbank estate was gifted to James Campbell (c.1640-c.1730) by his father Sir Hugh Campbell (d.1686, Edinburgh), on his marriage to Jean, daughter of Sir William Mure of Rowallan in 1672. The original house dates from this time, but was extended in 1838. In his *Journal of a Tour to the Hebrides*, with Samuel Johnson, James Boswell of Auchinleck, records calling on Mr. [James] Campbell, at Treesbank, *who was married to one of my wife's sisters*, on 30th October 1773. Although tenanted by others, the house remained in the Campbell family until at least 1911 when it was advertised for sale. Standing in 1,000 acres, it had the usual public rooms, seven bedrooms, three dressing rooms, bathrooms and a billiard room. There was a gravitation water supply, lighting by acetylene gas, stabling for ten horses, a coach house, garage and laundry, and two entrance lodges. It was purchased by the Kilmarnock carpet manufacturer, Gavin Morton of Blackwood Morton & Co., who commissioned the Ayr-based architect, James K Hunter, or possibly his assistant James Carrick (1880-1940), and between 1926 and 1928 the house was virtually rebuilt. Morton died in the house on 27th April 1954, at the age of 87 years. In 1974 it was bought by the Glasgow Trades Council and, at a cost of £400,000, converted to a residential training centre, opened by Len Murray, General Secretary of the TUC in October 1976. With accommodation for 35 students and conference facilities for 400, the centre operated until 1991 when it returned to private ownership.

Waterhaughs House, Darvel

Records of the early Waterhaughs House are scant, and details of its owners thin, nor can it be said with certainty who built it, or the adjacent farmhouse. In the 17th century it was owned by a family Campbell (a scion of the Campbells of Loudoun) but was forfeited by the Covenanter Matthew Campbell in the 1670s. The family was restored to the estate, the Register of Edinburgh Apprentices, 1701-1755 recording that Mungo Campbell, son to George Campbell of Waterhaughs was apprenticed to James Thom, druggist, in December 1720. On 15th March 1723, Marion Campbell of Waterhaughs married Nicholas Brown, said to have been a surgeon in Newmilns, and although it is not known when Mr. Brown became master of Waterhaughs, and later Lanfine, he was the first of a succession that ran until 1897, with the death of his niece Miss Martha Brown. With the completion of the building of Lanfine House in 1772, Waterhaughs housed its estate workers. As part of Lanfine, it was bought in 1911 by Sir Charles William Cayzer.

Wellwood House, Muirkirk

On the north bank of the River Ayr, two miles west of Muirkirk, Wellwood House shared a driveway with Middle Wellwood Farm, branching south off the road to Ayr at Haystackhill. The estate, with Over Wellwood and Under Wellwood, was in the hands of the Campbell family (heirs of Glaisnock) from the 16th century – a stone of the original house bore the inscription '1600 – TC.MC' – until 1787 when it was bought by the Duke of Portland, who exploited its coal reserves. In 1863 James Baird of Knoydart and Cambusdoon (1802-1876) bought the 17,566 acre estate, with its house and farms, for £135,000. He was succeeded by his nephew, John George Alexander Baird who, in 1878, built the house in this photograph. Born at Rosemount, Monkton in 1854, and educated at Eton he served five years with the army from 1877 (6th Dragoon Guards and 16th Lancers) and was Member of Parliament for Glasgow Central between 1886 and 1906. He was Honorary Colonel of the Ayrshire (Earl of Carrick's Own) Yeomanry and in November 1914 had eleven Belgian soldiers convalescing at Wellwood. Besides parliamentary duties and yeomanry interests he was active in local archaeology, publishing *An Account of the Excavation of Two Hut Circles at Muirkirk*, in 1914. Following his death, the house fell to neglect and decay and was demolished in April 1927. It is remembered in the poem *The Bonnie Lass o' Wellwood Ha'*, by the Muirkirk poet Thomas Floyd (1858-1933), and for the ghost of Beenie, a murdered servant girl, who left a bloody tread on an upper stairway.